Erika Knight

Simple Colour Knitting

A how-to-knit-with-colour workshop
with 20 desirable projects

photography by Yuki Sugiura

QUADRILLE

Publishing director Jane O'Shea
Commissioning editor Lisa Pendreigh
Editorial assistant Harriet Butt
Pattern checker Sally Harding
Creative director Helen Lewis
Art director and Designer Claire Peters
Photographer Yuki Sugiura
Stylist Holly Bruce
Model Chinh Hoang
Illustrator Claire Peters
Production director Vincent Smith
Production controller Stephen Lang

First published in 2015 by
Quadrille Publishing Ltd
Pentagon House
52–54 Southwark Street
London SE1 1UN
www.quadrille.co.uk

Quadrille is an imprint of Hardie Grant.
www.hardiegrant.com.au

Quadrille
craft

www.quadrillecraft.com

If you have any comments
or queries regarding the
instructions in this book,
please contact us at
enquiries@quadrille.co.uk

British Library Cataloguing-in-Publication
Data
A catalogue record for this book is available
from the British Library.

ISBN: 978 184949 271 3

Printed in China

 **Kirklees**
COUNCIL

Library and Information Centres

Red doles Lane

Huddersfield, West Yorkshire

HD2 1YF

This book should be returned on or before the latest date stamped below. Fines are charged if the item is late.

You may renew this loan for a further period by phone, personal visit or at www.kirklees.gov.uk/libraries, provided that the book is not required by another reader.

NO MORE THAN THREE RENEWALS ARE PERMITTED

Introduction

Colour evokes emotion. Colour affects our senses. Colour is a gauge of our mood. Colour conjures memories.

I have been designing palettes of colour for the fashion industry, and more specifically for knitwear and printed textiles, for much of my life. My fine art training instilled in me a love for the language of colour and its many dialects. Personally, my own colour palette tends towards natural shades and monochromes as a base with bright pops of colour to add energy and life.

Using colour within knitting to create interesting stitches, patterns and textiles is one of the most exciting aspects of the craft. This book is a glimpse into my creative process; how I look at, select and use colour. Rather than being an exhaustive tome on colour science or every colour knitting technique, instead Simple Colour Knitting is my personal view on colour. This book is more of a 'workbox', designed to inspire a diverse, versatile and 'big brush' approach to colour.

Simple Colour Knitting is about ways of incorporating colour in your knitting, with practical advice from techniques of plying, phasing, slipping stitches, stranding, colour blocking, embroidering and embellishing to more expressive approaches. Throughout this book the twenty projects build in skill level and provide a base to practise, experiment and create with colour. My hope it that it will inspire confidence in your own selections of colour and methods of using it.

We must hold on to our individuality through our creative endeavours, most especially our hand knits. Key to this is the 'handcrafted'. A craft that comes from the hand is for me the greatest form of creativity; honest, authentic and personal. Show your true colours. Add colour to your knitting.

In reality, all the projects in this book are unashamedly simple – that's my style. However, each project has been attributed with a skill level in accordance with the Craft Yarn Council of America's rating system in order to let you know what techniques you are mastering.

BEGINNER

1 Beginner Projects For first-time knitters using basic knit and purl stitches. Minimal shaping.

EASY

2 Easy Projects Using basic stitches, repetitive stitch patterns, simple colour changes and simple shaping and finishing.

INTERMEDIATE

3 Intermediate Projects With a variety of stitches, such as basic cables and lace, simple intarsia, knitting-in-the-round techniques, mid-level shaping and finishing.

EXPERIENCED

4 Experienced Projects Using advanced techniques and stitches, such as short rows, Fair Isle, more intricate intarsia, cables, lace patterns and numerous colour changes.

Inspiration

A ripe fig, a slick of oil on water, a patch of lichen on a rock, weathered paint on a wooden table. Inspiration cannot be prescriptive, it is instinctive and individual. The ways in which you may respond to that inspiration are many and varied, but finding it can sometimes seem a daunting task. Eliminate the white page. Take a walk. Visit a gallery. Go to a market. It's all about looking. Learn from what you see, trusting your eye and your judgement.

Source. Collect. Collate. Photograph. Play. Record. Draw. Paint. Crayon. Cut out. Alter. Photocopy. Reduce. Enlarge. Distort. Repeat.

The perfect colourway for a throw or a muffler may already exist within your favourite image, torn from a magazine and pinned to your noticeboard. Match the colours in that favourite image, painting, postcard or fabric to shades of yarn and wind off those onto a strip of card. Whilst I was at art school, a tutor once said to me, "It always comes back to landscape." When I am in in need of inspiration, it invariably does.

There are simple ways of producing personal, colourful and creative designs from the many and plentiful sources that fill our lives and experiences. I hope that the projects in this book will inspire and encourage you to be brave with colour, and to use your own personal response to colours in your knitting. There are no rights and wrongs with colour, only an understanding of how to use it to maximum effect.

Use the basics of the colour wheel as shown over the next pages, then invent and experiment with your own palettes:

Red life force, physical, passion, festivity, dominance
Blue sky and sea, workers, eternity, uniform, change, tranquility, new beginnings, durable, trust, loyalty
Yellow energy, power, precious, sacred, optimism, youth
Green nature, life, harmony, calming, everlasting, faith
Pink romance, fidelity, compassion, action, confidence
Purple regal, mystery, enlightenment, comfort, nostalgia
Orange ambition, generosity, vibrancy, happiness, energy
Black timeless, practical, spiritual, urban, confident
White pure, integrity, clarity, spiritual, fresh, peace
Naturals grounded, stable, secure, the perfect foil to accent or play with colour; a base on which to build

colour theory

Explaining our response to colour is as much about quantifying an emotional reaction as it is explaining an exact science.

Johannes Itten, a prominent teacher at the Bauhaus, produced the 'colour wheel' in its most recognisable form. He used blocks of primary, secondary and tertiary colours to form a wheel of twelve segments. Visually, each of the segments represents a colour and the wheel as a whole represents their circular relationship.

The principle of the colour wheel is that there are three PRIMARY colours: red, yellow and blue. They are primary as they exist alone and cannot be made up of any other colour.

Mixing primary colours in equal proportions creates SECONDARY colours; red and yellow create orange, blue and yellow create green, and red and blue make violet.

The remaining six segments on the colour wheel show the TERTIARY colours, which result from mixing adjacent and secondary colours in a ratio of 2:1 to produce red-orange, yellow-orange, yellow-green, blue-green, blue-purple and red-purple.

Black and white are not strictly classified as colours, and do not appear on the colour wheel.

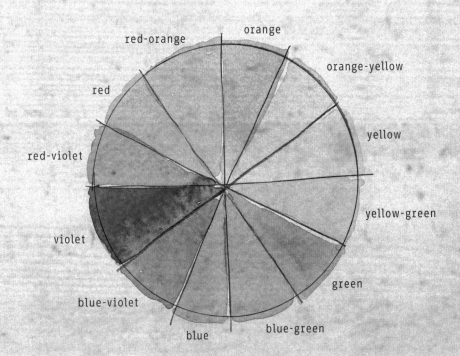

Whether you are selecting colours for the striped blanket or the tweed stitch scarf, the simplicity of the colour wheel is a fun tool for devising a colourway for a project.

On the following pages, four of the most useful ways of employing the colour wheel to create a colourway are explained: complementary or 'opposites attract'; analogous or 'next-to's'; split complementary or 'triangular'; monochromatic or 'ombré'.

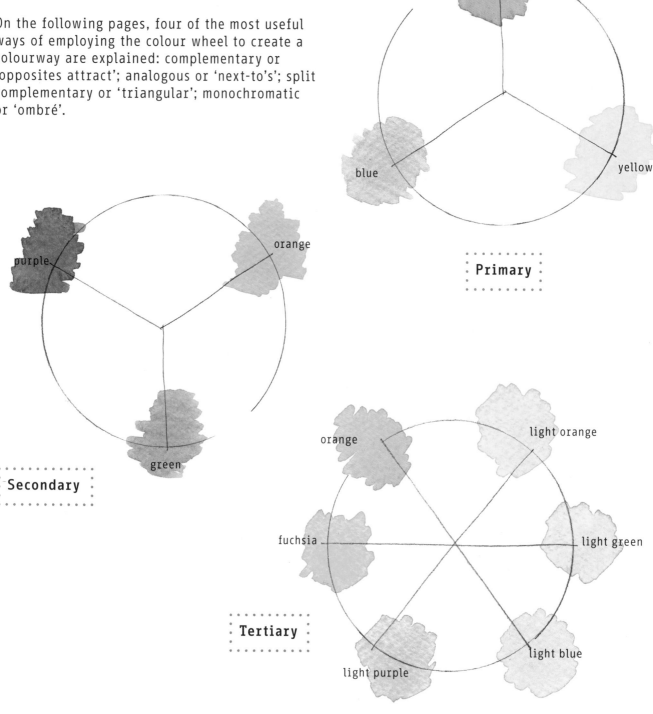

red

blue

yellow

Primary

orange

purple

green

Secondary

orange

light orange

fuchsia

light green

light purple

light blue

Tertiary

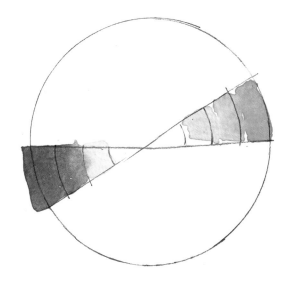

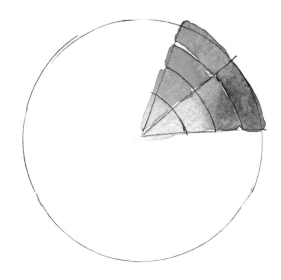

Opposites attract

Any two hues positioned directly opposite each other on the colour wheel are considered to be complementary colours. This always creates a dynamic energy, which is why I refer to them as 'opposites attract', and has great impact when used in moderation in a design. Blue with orange, red with green and yellow with purple, for example. When they are placed next to each other they make the other appear more intense and brighter. That's because, being opposite, one colour is always cool and the other is always warm with the greatest contrast.

I have used this simple colour principle in another way for the Faux Sheepskin Throw (see page 60). The natural wool 'fur' yarn in vibrant purple is styled with a brilliant yellow upholstered chair, creating a dynamic focus for a living room.

Next-to's

Colours that sit next to each other on the colour wheel are known as analogous, or as I simply call them 'next-to's'. Basically, this colour scheme features three or more hues, which are positioned next to each other on the colour wheel. Just choose any colour on the wheel as your main colour, then simply add the two or three colours next to it on either side of it. They all share similarities at their source and will easily harmonise. Next-to colour schemes are often found in nature and well, if it works in the natural world, it should look good on a bit of knitted fabric.

You may have a few balls of the main colour in your stash from a bargain or just 'had to have it' moment at the yarn store. So this is a good way to extend into a bigger project.

This does create a simple and successful colourway. These bright hues do work together and create a harmonious effect and are fab for kids knits, but maybe use a softer tone of one or two of the colours if a little more sophistication is required. Make sure you have enough contrast when choosing an analogous colour scheme. Maybe choose one colour to dominate, a second to support. The third colour is used (along with black, white or grey) as an accent.

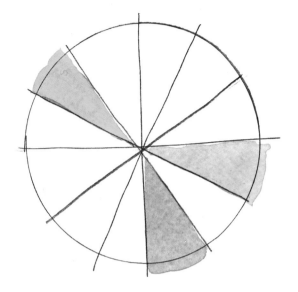

Triangular

A split complementary colour scheme is made up of three hues. First, pick your main colour. Next, go directly across to its complementary colour on the colour wheel. Don't pick this, but select the two colours either side of the complementary colour. For example, if you start with red, the colour opposite is green, but don't use this, instead use the yellow-green and blue-green either side.

Wherever you begin, there will always be at least one tertiary colour in your selection. As tertiary colours are blends, the final palette will be sophisticated with subtle mixes.

I organise my yarn stash in groups according to colour. The differing weights and textures add another dimension and aid the process of design. There are basic lessons to learn from colour theory, but do not assume that colours will always work together exactly as intended; go with the flow, experiment and be pleasantly surprised. All too often, selecting even a single shade for a project is tricky, let alone choosing three or more colours to work together. The one thing I have learnt along the way is that a colour can look very different when combined with others. It is always essential to 'swatch' up colours as they look different when knitted up as opposed to in the ball or hank.

Hand dyes
Your colour inspiration may come all in one hank of yarn, where the hand dyer has done the work for you. Beautiful contrasts, harmonies and tonal effects can be achieved in a single continuous thread of multi-coloured or hand-dyed yarn. Use it on its own or to add further depth to a Fair Isle as the background to accent colours. Alternatively, use stitch patterns that break the straight row and create further colour effects, such as a 'slip stitch'.

Tones

Black and white are not strictly classified as colours. They do not appear on the colour wheel. But black and white used simply together, I find, give great energy. I always use this colour combination in every collection. Black and white is always classic, always coveted.

Adding black or white to a colour will make a range of tints, tones and shades. If a colour is made lighter by adding white, the result is called a tint. If black is added, the darker version is called a shade. And if grey is added the result will be a different tone.

My personal favourite project in this book is monochromatic – using different tints, shades or tones of one colour together in one project. This is a very comfortable and safe choice. I have taken three fabulous hand dyes in blue, ranging from a dark indigo shade through a hue of denim blue to a tint of light chambray to create a further ombré effect by further plying the yarns and phasing the colours to knit a simple garter stitch throw and create a dip-dyed effect (see page 68).

The monochromatic colour scheme creates quite a sophisticated effect, maybe a beautiful variation to a solid colour knit and indeed many variations, obvious and some subtle, can be achieved from just one colour in this way.

tint   hue   shade

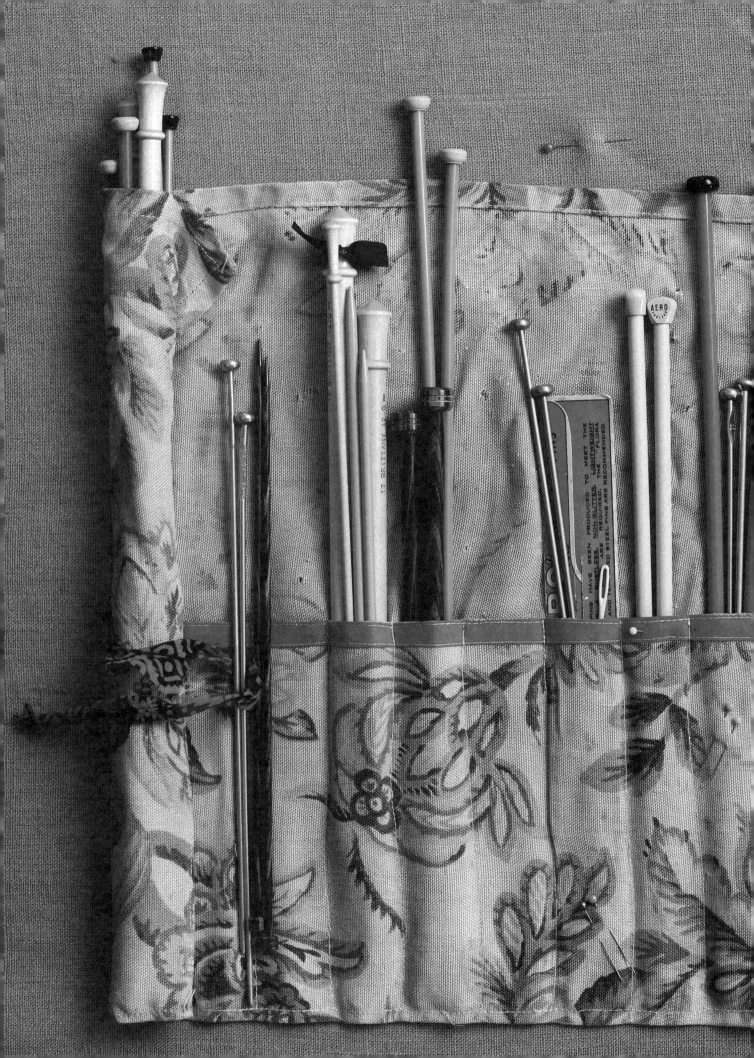

colour techniques

Plying & Phasing

Plying and phasing are two very simple techniques to inject colour into your knitting. By using two or more balls of different shades of yarn, but held together and worked with as if they were one yarn, you can create some simple yet stunning colour effects.

Create a washed denim effect by using varying tones of blue yarn.

Plying

Play around with different effects when plying together yarns to create energetic and individual effects. Try using a bulky yarn plied together with a strand of fine yarn. Combine a matt yarn, such as a cotton, with shiny yarn, such as mercerised cotton or viscose.

Create strong colour contrasts or more subtle effects to mimic the appearance of hand-dyed yarns.

To estimate the amount of yarn required for a project, knit up a small swatch, then unravel it and measure the length of yarn to guesstimate the amount of yarn needed for the size of the finished pieces.

Take care not to 'split' the yarn. Make sure you always work the strands together when working a stitch.

Take one strand of colour A + one strand of colour B and use them both together as one yarn.

Phasing

Use a sticky note to mark the actual row you are working on to avoid any confusion.

An ombré or phased effect can be created by using three or more colours of yarn.

Stripes in stocking stitch make a clean line on the knit side and a 'broken' stripe on the purl side.

On garter stitch stripes I especially like the 'wrong side' of the fabric.

Rib stitch stripes create a lively textile enhanced by the 'colour change' stitch peeking through.

Personally I favour odd-row stripes and even single row stripes, although this results in more ends to weave in.

Striping

Stripes may be any width and colour sequence you like: even or odd numbers of rows, the same colour sequence repeated, alternating widths or colours... the choice is yours. Horizontal stripes are the easiest way of working with two or more colours.

Take colour inspiration from a postcard of a favourite painting, ceramic or home textile... even a magazine cutting. Match the chosen colours from the inspirational image to yarns, then wind lengths of each yarn around a strip of card to create pleasing colour combinations and proportions (see pages 8–9). Referring to the inspiration strip, knit an individual textile imitating the proportions of colour and stripes.

If working wide stripes, cut the yarn at the end of each stripe. If working thinner or even-row stripes, the yarn can be carried up the side to avoid extra darning or weaving in later

It's easy to work odd-row stripes on double-pointed needles or a circular needle.

Joining a new colour at the beginning of a row

1 When changing colour or joining in a new ball – on the row before you need the new colour, work to the last stitch.

2 Taking the end of the new colour, use it together with the yarn in work to work the last stitch, creating a 'double stitch'.

3 On the first stitch of the next row, work the double stitch as one stitch with just the end of the new colour. This will securely 'anchor' your new yarn and not create unsightly knots or bumps.

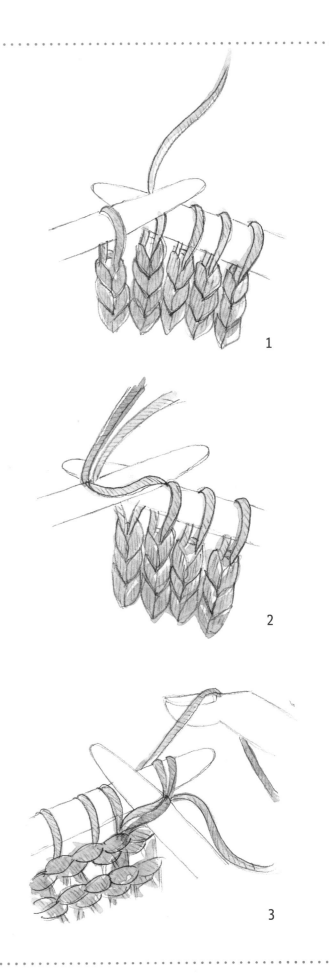

1

2

3

Stranding

Fair Isling or Fair Isle is a general term used for multi-coloured stocking stitch patterns. Authentic Fair Isles are very colourful with small motifs, often personal to the knitter, repeated across a row, using only two colours – one always carried at the back of the fabric, thus creating a double-thick fabric perfect for the cold Northern European climate where these were first created.

There are two methods used when working Fair Isle patterns – stranding the unused yarn all across the wrong side of the knitting, and weaving the two yarns together on the wrong side to avoid long loops of yarn.

Stranding one-handed

Stranding with one hand involves dropping one yarn after use, then picking up another and carrying it across the back of the work. It is important not to twist the yarns in the changeover between colours.

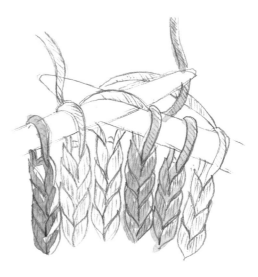

On a right-side (knit) row Using the first colour, knit three stitches. Drop the yarn and pick up the second colour, carrying it over the dropped yarn, and knit three stitches. Drop the second colour.

Pick up the first colour from underneath the second and bring it across the back of the last three knitted stitches. Knit the next three stitches, being careful not to pull the yarn too tight.

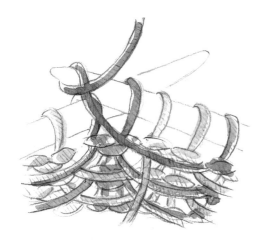

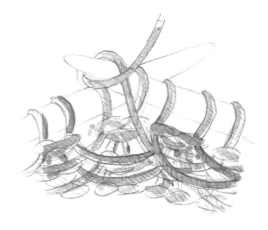

On a wrong-side (purl) row Using the first colour, purl three stitches. Drop the yarn and pick up the second colour, carrying it across the last three stitches over the top of the dropped colour. Purl three stitches. Drop the second colour.

Pick up the first colour from underneath the second, bring it across, and purl three stitches. Keep the stitches spread out along the right needle to avoid puckering.

Stranding two-handed

Using the stranding technique with two hands is faster than using just one, since the yarns do not need to be dropped between colour changes. Hold one colour over the forefinger of the left hand as for the continental knitting method, and the other according to the style in which you knit in the right hand.

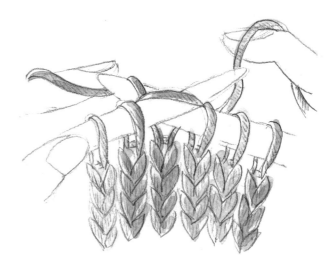

On a right-side (knit) row * Using the first colour, which is held in the right hand, knit three stitches.

Using your left hand, bring the second colour across the back of the work, over the top of the first yarn and knit the next three stitches in the continental style. Repeat from * to end.

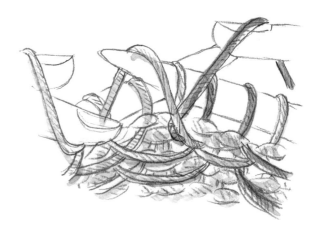

On a wrong-side (purl) row Hold the first colour over the left forefinger and the second yarn in your right hand. Purl three stitches in the second colour, carrying it over the last three stitches.

Using the first yarn and the continental method, purl the next three stitches.

Weaving

If a colour needs to be carried across the back of the work over more than three stitches, it will need to be caught or woven in. It is best to do this every second or third stitch, since weaving on every stitch can distort the shape of the knitted stitch and weaving too infrequently creates loops. As with stranding, weaving can be done using either the one-handed or two-handed method.

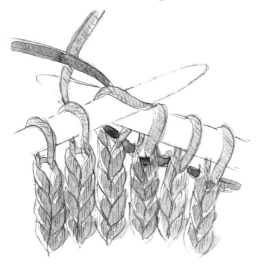

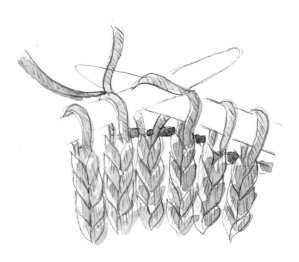

On a right-side (knit) row Work to the point where the second colour needs to be caught in. Bring the second colour up from under the one in use and over the right needle and your left forefinger from right to left.

Using the right needle, knit the stitch, dropping the stitch and the carried yarn from the left needle as you do so. Hold the carried yarn in place at the back of the work, using your left forefinger, and continue to knit using the first colour.

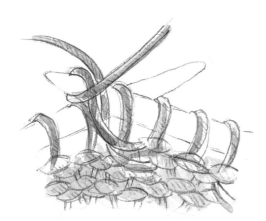

On a wrong-side (purl) row Work to the point where the second colour needs to be caught in. Bring the second colour up from under the one in use and around the right needle from right to left, anchoring it in place with your left thumb at the front of the work.

Using the right needle, purl the next stitch, taking care not to take the carried colour through the stitch. Continue to purl following the pattern.

Colour Blocking

With colour blocking any number of colours can be used in a single row to create a placed motif or picture. There is no need to strand or weave on the wrong side of the knitting, as individual colours are introduced as and when they are required within the row using a separate ball of yarn to create a single fabric.

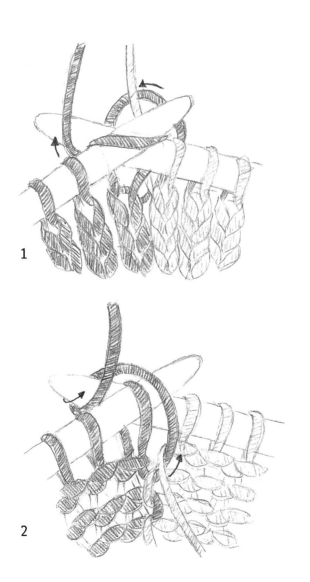

1

2

Changing yarn using the colour-block (intarsia) method

When knitting using several colours across a row, organise the yarns into small balls or 'bobbins' – small windings of individual yarns. To work out how much yarn you will need, calculate the number of stitches in that specific area then twist the yarn around the knitting needle that number of times, adding a small amount more for sewing in the ends. Once you have measured out the correct amount of yarn, either wind it into a small bobbin by hand or wrap it around a shop-bought bobbin.

1 To change to a new colour on a knit row, work up to the colour change. Drop the old colour. Pick up the new colour from under the old colour and knit to the next colour change.

2 On a purl row, work up to the colour change. Drop the old colour. Pick up the new colour from under the old colour and purl to the next colour change.

In effect, you are 'twisting' the two colours around each other to link them together. Be careful not to overtwist the yarn or the fabric will not lie flat. The object is to link together the two separate colour sections so that they form a single fabric.

Working from charts

Colour patterns are often worked from charts and the colours are indicated by either coloured squares or symbols within each square.

Each square represents a stitch and each row of squares represents a row of knitting. The patterns are worked in stocking stitch, i.e. one row knit, one row purl alternately, unless otherwise stated.

Read the knit rows (usually odd-numbered) from right to left and read the purl rows (usually even-numbered) from left to right (unless otherwise instructed by the pattern). Continue to work on this principle until the design is completed.

Square Motif
- use a separate ball of yarn for each area of colour

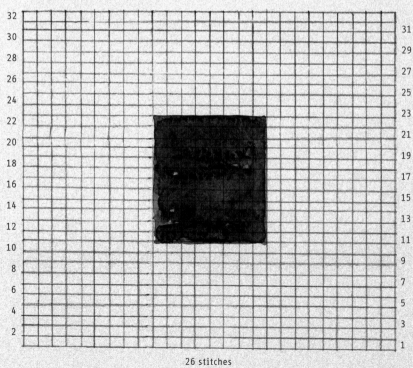

26 stitches

Embroidering

Swiss darning or duplicate stitch is a form of embroidery made to look like knit stitches. Using a blunt-tipped sewing needle and yarn, you can sew small areas of colour over the top of knitted stitches to add decorative detail without having to use the tricky technique of knitting with multiple colours.

Take inspiration from fabrics – simply photocopy the fabric, reduce or enlarge the image as required and trace it onto graph paper. Use needlepoint designs as inspiration, too.

Adapt the outline of the design you have chosen to fit the squares or photocopy directly onto knitters chart paper, simplifying the areas of 'tones' of colour. Remember that each square on the graph or chart paper represents one stitch.

Once your design is on the chart, follow it to Swiss darn the motif on top of your knitting.

To knit each of the coloured stitches that make up the rose motif on the Plaid Rose Cushion (see pages 138–141) would be incredibly difficult and challenge even the most proficient knitter. I think you get a far better result by embroidering the odd highlight colour over a base colour. But do make sure when you are Swiss darning over the top of the knitted stitches, not to pull the embroidered stitches too tight as this will pucker the fabric.

Mark the section you are going to start embroidering with pins (1).

Thread a large blunt-tipped needle with yarn of the same ply as the background. Secure by working two or three stitches on top of one another at the back of the first stitch. Insert the needle from the back to the front, through the base of the first stitch. Thread the needle from right to left under the two vertical loops of the same stitch, but one row above (2).

Gently pull the yarn through; a stitch is formed covering the right-hand vertical top loop of the knitted stitch. Then re-insert the needle ino the base of the stitch to be covered, and then out to the front again through the base of the next stitch to the left (3).

Pull the yarn through; one Swiss darned stitch is now complete. Do not pull the yarn too tightly; the darning must be the same tension as the background.

To complete the first line of a block of colour, continue working from right to left along a row for the number of stitches required. The stitches should all be flat and even.

It is easier to work the second and alternate rows if you turn the knitting upside down. This is so that the stitches are always worked in the same direction.

1

2

3

Slipping Stitches

Slipping stitches is one of the simplest ways of putting colour into your knitting. If you are concerned about working with more than one colour at a time, this is the technique for you as only one colour is used in each row.

The tweed stitch used in the Muffler Scarf on page 92 is a good example of a simple slip-stitch colour pattern. It is slow to knit but produces a flat woven-like fabric. You may find it easier to work this stitch on a larger size needle than the one suggested in the pattern.

The tweed stitch also creates a versatile and attractive double-sided textile. Worked in three colours, it requires a dark (A), medium (B) and a light (C) colour to give a good contrast. My favourite combination is simply black, grey and ecru (light fawn).

Tip To try out the tweed stitch, cast on an odd number of stitches and work the stitch following the instructions on page 93. If you aren't certain which colour to use next when working the stitch stitch, pick up the colour at the beginning of the needles, two rows below the 'working' stitches.

Slipping a stitch purlwise

When a slip-stitch colour pattern simply instructs you to slip one or more stitches, without specifying how you should do this, it means that the stitches are to be slipped purlwise.

To slip a stitch purlwise on a knit row, first insert the tip of the right needle, from right to left, through the front loop of the next stitch on the left needle. Keep the yarn at the back of the work unless your instructions state otherwise. You will have inserted the right needle as if you were about to work a purl stitch, but instead, you slip the stitch onto the right needle. The slipped stitch now sits on the right needle with the right side of the loop at the front, like the worked stitches next to it.

Slip a stitch on a purl row in the same way, but keep the yarn at the front of the work unless your instructions state otherwise.

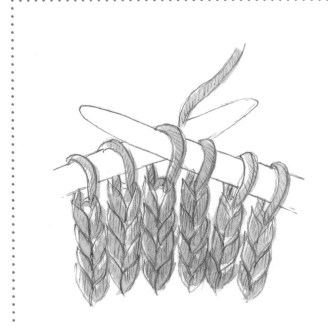

Finishing

When all the knitted pieces are done,
take time to finish...

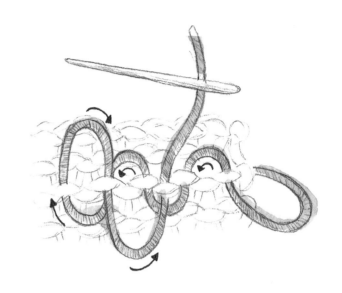

Ends

To sew in yarn ends, use a blunt-tipped needle to
'weave' each end in separately across the knitting
on the wrong side (never along the edges) for
about four stitches, then back one to two stitches
to hold the end firmly in place.

This technique is especially good for cotton,
linens and hemps as due to their 'plant' nature
they are non-elastic and tend to unravel.

Picking up stitches

You may sometimes need to pick up and knit
stitches along the edge of your knitting, for
example to add on a knitted edging. To pick up
stitches evenly, divide the edge into regular
sections with pins placed at right angles to the
edge, then divide the total number of stitches
required by the number of sections. Pick up that
number of stitches between each pin.

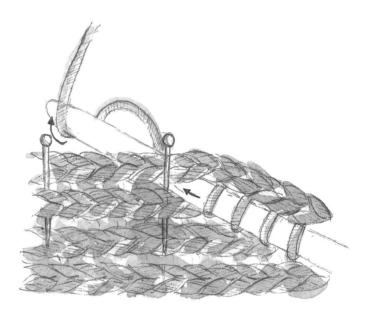

Along row ends
Use pins to mark the row ends along the selvedge,
evenly spacing the pins at the end of every four
rows, as shown here. Pick up and knit three
stitches between each pair of pins, inserting
the needle into the centre of the edge stitch,
wrapping the yarn around the tip of the needle
and drawing the yarn through to create a loop on
the needle.

Along a curved edge
On most armhole borders and neckbands you will
need to pick up stitches along a curved edge. As
a general rule, pick up one stitch in each cast-off
stitch and three for every four row ends. For a
smooth edge, do not pick up corner stitches on
stepped decreases.

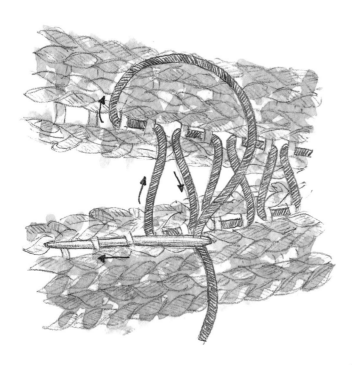

Invisible seams are used to join all side and sleeve seams, or where a flat seam with no bulk is required.

With the right side of both pieces facing you, secure the yarn to the edge of one piece. Take the needle across to the opposite edge, pick up the equivalent stitch on this piece, pull the yarn through; take the needle back to the first edge, returning the needle through the hole of the previous stitch, then pick up the next stitch and pull the yarn through.

Continue in this way picking up and pulling together stitch to stitch (row for row) along the length of the seam.

Once you have mastered this, you will never look back.

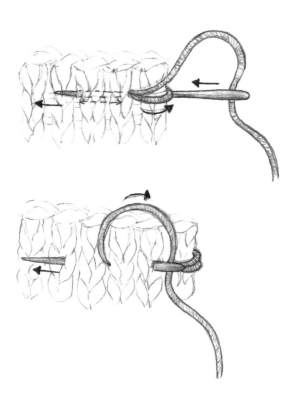

Backstitch seam

A backstitch seam is used where a firm edge is required to hold the shape, such as a set-in sleeve, or to give strength at any point where the garment may take extra strain. It can also be used as a decorative feature of the design, for cushions, etc.

Place the pieces with the right sides together. Work along the wrong side of the fabric one stitch from the edge.

Secure the yarn and work from right to left. With the needle at the back of the work move along to the left the length of one knitted stitch, bring the needle through fabric to front and pull the yarn through. Take the needle from left to right across front of work to the end of last stitch, insert the needle through the fabric to the back of the work and pull the yarn through. Continue in this way.

Blocking

The process of pinning and pressing knitted pieces is called blocking and it will make your finished projects look as good as possible. First sew in the yarn ends, then steam or wet press as appropriate.

Block and pin

To block a piece of knitting, pin it out to the correct size and shape on your irongin board or a padded surface (a table covered with a folded blanket under a sheet is ideal). Pin each piece, wrong side facing up. Do not stretch or distort the fabric. Make sure all the rows run in straight lines. Check that the width and length of each piece match the measurements given on the pattern. Pin closely around the edge of each piece of knitting, placing pins at right angles to the edges.

Steam pressing

This method is used for natural yarns or those with a high wool content. Care should be taken with long-haired fibres, such as mohair and angora, or items with textured stitches, to ensure the steaming process does not matt the fibres or flatten the pattern. Check the information on the yarn label and test-press a tension square first if you have any doubts.

Use rustproof large-headed pins to pin out each piece to its exact measurements as explained above. Lay a clean cotton cloth over your pinned knitting to protect it.

Set the iron to an appropriate heat setting for your yarn. Hold the iron close to the cotton cloth and allow the steam to permeate. Do not press the iron onto the knitted fabric. Remove the cloth and allow the knitting to dry before unpinning.

Wet pressing

This method is suitable for synthetics and fancy yarns. Pin out your knitting as for steam pressing. Wet a clean cloth and squeeze out the excess water until it is just damp. Place the cloth over your knitting and leave to dry. Remove the cloth when it is completely dry and ensure the knitted pieces are also dry before unpinning them.

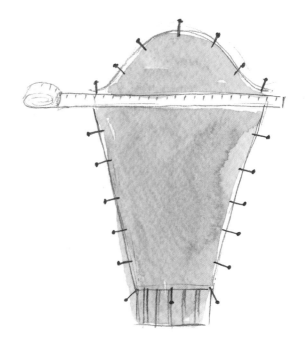

swatch gallery

opposites attract

Colours on opposing sides of the colour wheel (see page 12) always provide a vibrant contrast, one colour is always cool whilst the other is always warm. When contrasting or complementary colours are adjacent they make each other appear brighter and more intense.

Worked over any number of stitches

Horizontal bands of contrasting colour worked in stocking stitch.

Worked over any number of stitches

Vertical bands of contrasting colour worked in stocking stitch using the colour-blocking (intarsia) technique (see page 32).

Bright Pink + Bright Green

- *experiment with opposing colours*

Orange + Blue

- *cast on and cast off a scarf in contrasting colours*

Purple + Yellow

- contrasting colours create energy

Worked over any number of stitches

Vertical bands of contrasting colour worked in stocking stitch and reverse stocking stitch alternately using the colour-blocking (intarsia) technique (see page 32).

Black + Neutral

- not strictly on the colour wheel but never to be ignored

Worked over any number of stitches

Horiztonal bands of contrasting colour worked in reverse stocking stitch.

plying and phasing

Individual effects are created using two or more colours as one yarn. This 'make do and mend' technique disguises any shortage when a substitute yarn is introduced.

Worked over any number of stitches, using colours A and B

Work in stocking stitch (K 1 row, P 1 row alternately), using one end of A and one end of B held together.

Plied Stocking Stitch
– one strand of colour A and one strand of colour B held together

Worked over any number of stitches, using colours A and B

Work in reverse stocking stitch (P 1 row, K 1 row alternately), using one end of A and one end of B held together.

Plied Reverse Stocking Stitch
– the random texture and colour of the reverse side looks equally good

Ombré Garter Stitch
– creates a subtle colour effect akin to hand-dyed yarns

Worked over any number of stitches, using colours A, B and C

Knit every row following the colour sequence below:
6 rows in A
2 rows in B
2 rows in A
2 rows in B
2 rows in A
8 rows in B
2 rows in C
2 rows in B
2 rows in C
2 rows in B
7 rows in B

Ombré Garter Stitch
– a dip-dye effect can be created using three or more colours

Worked over any number of stitches, using colours A, B and C

Knit every row following the colour sequence below with the two yarn ends held together:
4 rows in A+A
5 rows in A+B
5 rows in B+B
5 rows in B+C
4 rows in C+C

striping

Stripes are a simple, effective and varied way to add interest to knitting. Stripes can be vibrant or subtle, regular or random. Use as many colours as your yarn stash or your imagination allow.

Worked over any number of stitches, using colours A and B

Row 1 (RS) Using A, knit.
Row 2 Using A, purl.
Rows 3 and 4 Rep rows 1 and 2.
Row 5 Using A, knit.
Row 6 Using B, knit.
Rep these 6 rows.

Purl Bar Stripe
- fine purl bar stripes create subtle interest

Worked over any number of stitches, using colours A and B

Row 1 (RS) Using A, knit.
Row 2 Using A, purl.
Row 3 (RS) Using B, knit.
Row 4 Using B, purl.
Rep these 4 rows.

Even-Row Stripes
- even-row stripes in two colours are easy to knit and always classic

Diagonal Stripes
- this technique always produces a square of knitting, so creating a diagonal is easy

Start with 2 stitches and work using colours A, B and C

Using A, cast on 2 sts.
Row 1 (RS) K1, K into front and back of last st (called *inc*).
3 sts.
Row 2 K2, inc in last st. *4 sts.*
Row 3 K to last st, inc in last st. *5 sts.*
Rep row 3 until there are 32 sts on needle.
Next row K.
Next row (dec) K to last 2 sts, K2tog. *31 sts.*
Rep last row until 26 sts rem.
Cont to dec as set, working stripes as follows:
2 rows in C
2 rows in A
4 rows in B
2 rows in A
2 rows in C
Using A, cont to dec as set until 2 sts rem.
Next row K2tog and fasten off.

Multi-Colour Stripes
- vary the row size of stripes to create an individual pattern

Worked over any number of stitches, using five colours – A, B, C, D and E

Beg with a P row, work in st st stripes as follows:
*3 rows in A
2 rows in B
2 rows in C
2 rows in B
[1 row in D, 1 row in E] 7 times
1 row in D
2 rows in B
2 rows in C
2 rows in B
3 rows in A
Rep from *.

slipping stitches

In slip-stitch colour patterns one colour is used in each row and stitches are slipped (purlwise) to take the colour over two rows (see page 36).

Worked over a multiple of 2 sts + 1 st extra, using colours A and B

Row 1 (RS) Using A, K1, *sl 1, K1; rep from * to end.
Row 2 Using A, K1, *yf, sl 1, yb, K1; rep from * to end.
Row 3 Using B, K2, *sl 1, K1; rep from * to last st, K1.
Row 4 Using B, K2, *yf, sl 1, yb, K1; rep from * to last st, K1.
Rep these 4 rows.

Moss Slip Stitch
- this stitch works well for a cushion as it is firm with straight edges

Worked over a multiple of 6 sts + 2 sts extra, using colours A, B, C and D

Row 1 (RS) Using A, K.
Row 2 Using A, P.
Row 3 Using B, K2, *sl 4, K2; rep from * to end.
Row 4 Using B, P3, sl 2, *P4, sl 2; rep from * to last 3 sts, P3.
Rows 5 and 6 Using B, rep rows 1 and 2.
Row 7 Using C, K1, sl 2, K2, *sl 4, K2; rep from * to last 3 sts, sl 2, K1.
Row 8 Using C, P1, sl 1, P4, *sl 2, P4; rep from * to last 2 sts, sl 1, P1.
Rows 9 and 10 Using C, rep rows 1 and 2.
Rows 11 and 12 Using D, rep rows 3 and 4.
Rows 13 and 14 Using D, rep rows 1 and 2.
Rows 15 and 16 Using A, rep rows 7 and 8.
Rep these 16 rows.

Slip Stitch Diamonds
- a favourite stitch for its vintage look. I call it 'Cheat's Fair Isle'

Slip Stitch Rib
- a non-elastic rib effect often used in Fair Isle sweaters

Worked over a multiple of 2 sts + 1 st extra, using colours A and B

Foundation row 1 (RS) Using A, K.
Foundation row 2 Using A, P.
Row 1 Using B, K1, *sl 1, K1; rep from * to end.
Row 2 Using B, P1, *sl 1, P1; rep from * to end.
Row 3 Using A, K2, sl 1, *K1, sl 1; rep from * to last 2 sts, K2.
Row 4 Using A, K2, sl 1, *P1, sl 1; rep from * to last 2 sts, P2.
Rep these 4 rows.

Tweed Stitch
- play with colours to see how they recede or dominate

Worked over a multiple of 2 sts + 1 st extra, using colours A, B and C

Set-up row (WS) Using A, P.
Row 1 (RS) Using B, K1, *yf, sl 1, yb, K1; rep from * to end.
Row 2 Using C, K1, P1, *yb, sl 1, yf, P1; rep from * to last st, K1.
Row 3 Using A, rep row 1.
Row 4 Using B, rep row 2.
Row 5 Using C, rep row 1.
Row 6 Using A, rep row 2.
Rep rows 1–6.

stranding

Created by stranding, where two colours are used in a single row, these patterns follow the colour sequences given in the charts. Drop the colour not in use and allow it to strand loosely across the back of the work.

Worked over any number of stitches, using colours A and B

Knit and purl alternate rows using the colour as indicated on the chart on page 101.

Worked over an even number of stitches, using colours A and B (but vary the colours you use for A and B if desired as shown here)

Every row [K1, P1] to end.

For two-colour rib, use one colour for knit and one colour for purl on row 1, keeping the same colours in the same stitches on subsequent rows to make vertical stripes, and always carrying the yarn on the wrong side of the fabric.

Houndstooth Pattern
- a classic pattern and a firm favourite

Bicolour Rib Pattern
- change the colours often to create an interesting textile with pronounced purl stitches

Worked over any number of stitches, using six colours – A, B, C, D, E and F

Knit all RS (odd-numbered) rows and purl all WS (odd-numbered) rows, using the colours as indicated on the chart.

Reading from a chart Read knit (RS) rows from right to left and read purl (WS) rows from left to right.

Fair Isle Pattern
*- endless colourways
are possible with
traditional patterns:
pastels are an especially
fresh alternative*

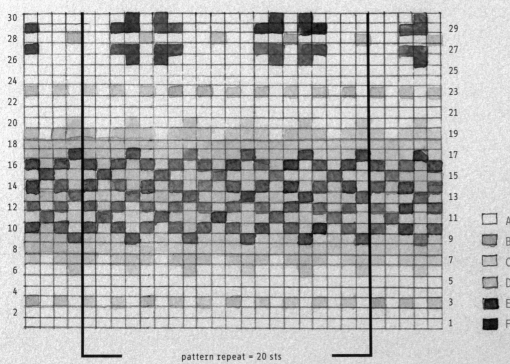

☐	A
▨	B
☐	C
▨	D
▧	E
■	F

pattern repeat = 20 sts

colour block motifs

With colour blocking, any number of colours can be used in a single row to create a placed motif or picture (see page 32).

Worked over any number of stitches, using colours A and B

Knit all RS (odd-numbered) rows and purl all WS (even-numbered) rows, using the colours as indicated on the chart.

Reading from a chart Read knit (RS) rows from right to left and read purl (WS) rows from left to right.

When working large areas of colour, use separate lengths or small balls of yarn for each area of colour and twist the strands of yarn at the back of the work when changing colours to avoid a hole.

Square Motif
- experiment with the same colour square motif but placed on different backgrounds

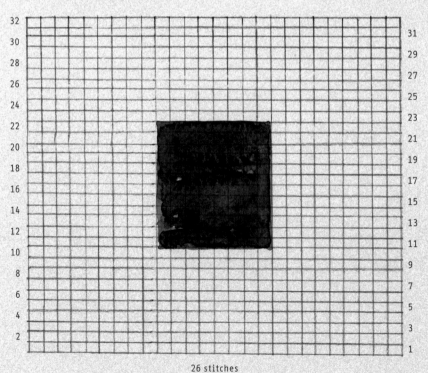

 A
☐ B

26 stitches

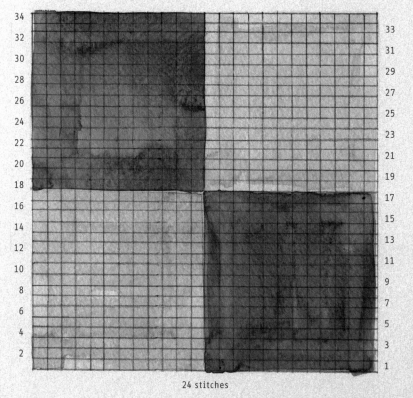

Chequerboard Motif
– an easy colourwork design for a beginner knitter that can be applied to any project

Worked over any number of stitches, using colours A and B

Knit all RS (odd-numbered) rows and purl all WS (even-numbered) rows, using the colours as indicated on the chart.

Reading from a chart Read knit (RS) rows from right to left and read purl (WS) rows from left to right.

When working large areas of colour, use separate lengths or small balls of yarn for each area of colour and twist the strands of yarn at the back of the work when changing colours to avoid a hole.

34
33
32
31
30
29
28
27
26
25
24
23
22
21
20
19
18
17
16
15
14
13
12
11
10
9
8
7
6
5
4
3
2
1

24 stitches

 A
B

colour block motifs

Worked over any number of stitches, using colours A and B

Knit all RS (odd-numbered) rows and purl all WS (even-numbered) rows, using the colours as indicated on the chart.

Reading from a chart Read knit (RS) rows from right to left and read purl (WS) rows from left to right.

When working large areas of colour, use separate lengths or small balls of yarn for each area of colour and twist the strands of yarn at the back of the work when changing colours to avoid a hole.

Spot Motif
— as an alternative, work each spot in a different colour

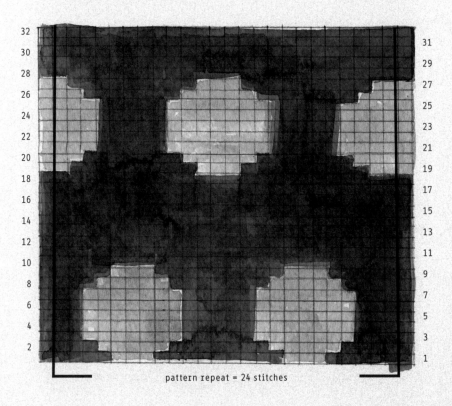

A

B

pattern repeat = 24 stitches

Random Motif
- create and
chart your own
motifs

Worked over any number of stitches, using colours A and B

Knit all RS (odd-numbered) rows and purl all WS (even-numbered) rows, using the colours as indicated on the chart.

Reading from a chart Read knit (RS) rows from right to left and read purl (WS) rows from left to right.

When working large areas of colour, use separate lengths or small balls of yarn for each area of colour and twist the strands of yarn at the back of the work when changing colours to avoid a hole.

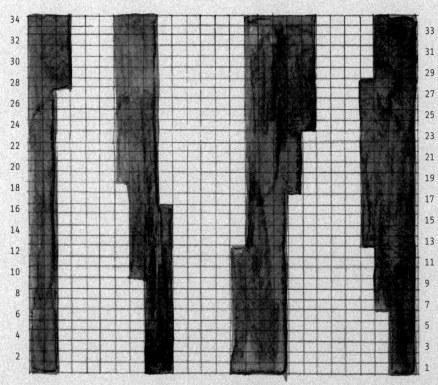

pattern repeat = 27 stitches

 A

☐ B

embellished motifs

Knitted fabric can be further embellished with embroidery, such as large areas of additional colour, motifs, pattern detail or vertical lines.

Worked over any number of stitches, using colours A, B and C

Knit and purl alternate rows working the horizontal stripes using the colour as indicated on the chart. When the knitting is complete, add the vertical stripes using Swiss darning (duplicate stitch) embroidery (see pages 34–35) in the colour shown on the chart.

Plaid Motif
- *any number of additional colours can be added in this way*

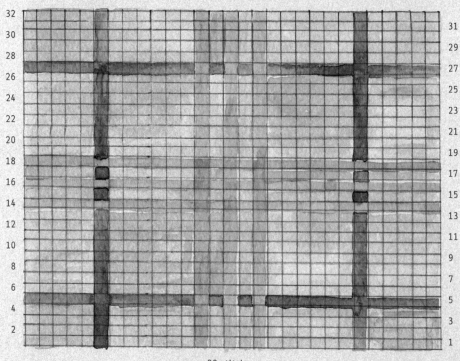

29 stitches

A
B
C

Worked over any number of stitches

Knit and purl alternate rows working the larger areas of base colour as indicated on the chart. When the knitting is complete, add the further detail colours using Swiss darning (duplicate stitch) embroidery (see pages 34–35) in the colour shown on the chart.

Rose Motif
- use a needlepoint or embroidery design for inspiration

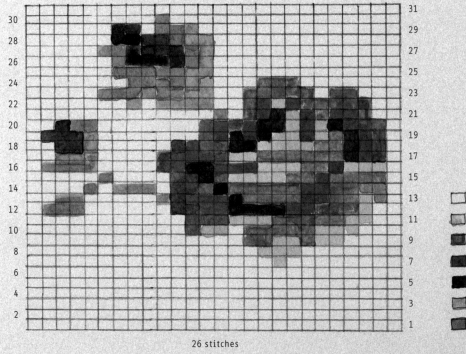

26 stitches

☐	A
☐	B
☐	C
☐	D
☐	E
☐	F
☐	G

project
workshops

1 Faux Sheepskin Throw

Made in pure wool 'fur' yarn, this sheepskin-shape throw is worked in simple garter stitch. It adds a striking and strong colour statement to a chair, couch or floor when two contrasting colours are 'brought together' or juxtaposed.

Skill level...

BEGINNER

In this project you will learn...
Increasing and decreasing

Stitches used...
Garter stitch (knit every row)

Materials
4 x 100g hanks of super-chunky-weight 'fur' yarn, such as Erika Knight *Fur Wool* (97% wool, 3% nylon binder; 40m/44yd per 100g/3½oz hank; 6 SUPER BULKY) in purple (Mulberry)
Pair of 12mm (US size 17) knitting needles
Large blunt-tipped sewing needle

Size
Approximately 92cm (36¾in) long and 54.5cm (21¾in) across widest point

Tension
5½ sts and 11 rows to 10cm (4in) square measured over garter stitch using 12mm (US size 17) needles. Use smaller or larger needles if necessary to obtain the correct tension.

Abbreviations
K2tog knit 2 sts together
See also page 143.

Note
Joining in a new ball
To achieve a neater finish, avoid joining in a new ball of yarn at the edge of your work.

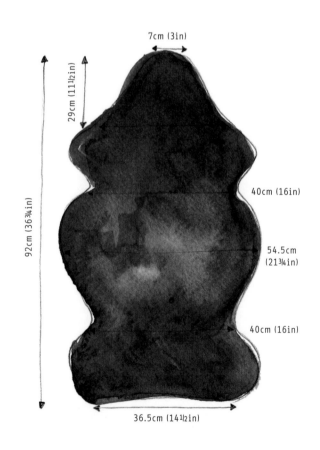

7cm (3in)

29cm (11½in)

92cm (36¾in)

40cm (16in)

54.5cm (21¾in)

40cm (16in)

36.5cm (14½in)

To make the throw
Cast on 20 sts and work in garter st (K every row) throughout as follows:
Row 1 K.
Row 2 Cast on 2 sts at beg of row, K to end. *22 sts.*
Row 3 Cast on 4 sts at beg of row, K to end. *26 sts.*
Row 4 Cast on 3 sts at beg of row, K to last 2 sts, K into front and back of next st, K1. *30 sts.*
Rows 5–13 K these 9 rows.
Row 14 K2tog, K to last 2 sts, K2tog. *28 sts.*
Rows 15–16 K these 2 rows.
Row 17 Rep row 14. *26 sts.*
Row 18 K.
Row 19 Rep row 14. *24 sts.*
Row 20 K.
Row 21 Rep row 14. *22 sts.*
Rows 22–25 K these 4 rows.
Row 26 K into front and back of first st, K to last 2 sts, K into front and back of next st, K1. *24 sts.*
Rows 27–28 K these 2 rows.
Row 29 Rep row 26. *26 sts.*
Rows 30–33 K these 4 rows.
Row 34 Rep row 26. *28 sts.*
Rows 35 K.
Row 36 Rep row 26. *30 sts.*
Rows 37–51 K these 15 rows.
Row 52 Rep row 14. *28 sts.*
Row 53 Rep row 14. *26 sts.*
Row 54 K.
Row 55 Rep row 14. *24 sts.*
Rows 56–58 K these 3 rows.
Row 59 Rep row 14. *22 sts.*
Rows 60–61 K these 2 rows.
Row 62 Rep row26. *24 sts.*
Row 63 K.

Row 64 Rep row 26. *26 sts.*
Row 65 K.
Row 66 Rep row 26. *28 sts.*
Row 67 K.
Row 68 Rep row 26. *30 sts.*
Rows 69–71 K these 3 rows.
Row 72 Rep row 14. *28 sts.*
Rows 73–74 K these 2 rows.
Row 75 Cast off 2 sts at beg of row, K to end. *26 sts.*
Row 76 Cast off 2 sts at beg of row, K to end. *24 sts.*
Rows 77–78 K these 2 rows.
Row 79 Rep row 14. *22 sts.*
Rows 80–82 K these 3 rows.
Row 83 Rep row 14. *20 sts.*
Rows 84–85 K these 2 rows.
Row 86 Rep row 14. *18 sts.*
Rows 87–88 K these 2 rows.
Row 89 Rep row 14. *16 sts.*
Row 90 K.
Row 91 Rep row 14. *14 sts.*
Rows 92–93 K these 2 rows.
Row 94 Rep row 14. *12 sts.*
Rows 95–96 K these 2 rows.
Row 97 Rep row 14. *10 sts.*
Row 98 K.
Row 99 Cast off 2 sts at beg of row, K to last 2 sts, K2tog. *7 sts.*
Row 100 Cast off 2 sts at beg of row, K to end. *5 sts.*
Row 101 K2tog, K to end. *4 sts.*
Cast off.

To finish
Weave in any loose yarn ends.

2 Plied Sweater

This basic raglan-sleeve sweater is knitted with a strand of two contrasting yarns 'plied' together. It can be sewn together so either the smooth side or the reverse side of the stocking stitch shows and is a great shared piece as the size range fits men and women.

Skill level

■■□□□
EASY

In this project you will learn…

Plying yarn

Stitches used

Stocking stitch; K1, P1 rib; increasing and decreasing

Materials

Super-chunky-weight wool yarn, such as Erika Knight *Maxi Wool* (100% British wool; 80m/87yd per 100g/3½oz hank; (6) SUPER BULKY) in the following colour:

    A off white (Canvas) – 7(7:8:8:9:10) hanks

Aran-weight wool yarn, such as Erika Knight *Vintage Wool* (100% pure British wool; 87m/95yd per 50g/1¾oz hank; (4) MEDIUM) in the following colour:

    B black (Pitch) – 6(6:7:7:8:9) hanks

Pair each of 10mm and 12mm (US sizes 15 and 17) knitting needles
12mm (US size 17) circular knitting needle, for neckband
Large blunt-tipped sewing needle

Tension

8½ sts and 11 rows to 10cm (4in) square measured over st st using 12mm (US size 17) needles and one strand of A and one strand of B held together. Use smaller or larger needles if necessary to obtain the correct tension.

Abbreviations

See page 143.

Size	XS	S	M	L	X	XXL
To fit chest (cm)	86	91	97	102	107	112
To fit chest (in)	34	36	38	40	42	44

Knitted measurements

	XS	S	M	L	X	XXL
Around chest (cm)	99	104	108	113	118	122
Around chest (in)	39½	41½	43	45	47	49
Length to shoulder (cm)	63.5	67	69	73	75	79
Length to shoulder (in)	25	26½	27¼	28¾	29¾	31¼
Sleeve seam (cm)	46	46	47	47	48	48
Sleeve seam (in)	18	18	18½	18½	19	19

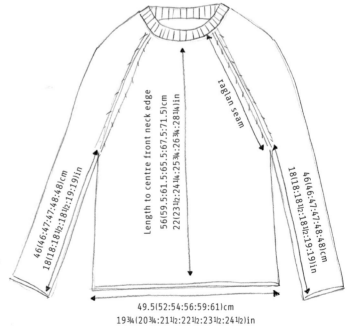

46(46:47:47:48:48)cm
18(18:18½:18½:19:19)in

Length to centre front neck edge
56(59.5:61.5:65.5:67.5:71.5)cm
22(23½:24¼:25¾:26¾:28¼)in

raglan seam

46(46:47:47:48:48)cm
18(18:18½:18½:19:19)in

49.5(52:54:56:59:61)cm
19¾(20¾:21½:22½:23½:24½)in

To make the sweater

Back

Using 10mm (US size 15) needles and one strand of A and one strand of B held tog, cast on 42(44:46:48:50:52) sts.

Beg with a K row, work 6 rows in st st.

Change to 12mm (US size 17) needles and cont in st st throughout, work until Back measures 40(42:44:46:48:50)cm/15¾(16½:17¼:18:19:19¾)in from cast-on edge, ending with RS facing for next row.

Shape raglan

Cast off 3 sts at beg of next 2 rows. *36(38:40:42:44:46) sts.*

Next row (dec on RS) K3, K2tog, K to last 5 sts, K2tog tbl, K3. *34(36:38:40:42:44) sts.*

Next row P.

Next row Dec 1 st at both ends of row as set. *32(34:36:38:40:42) sts.*

Next row (dec on WS) P3, P2tog tbl, P to last 5 sts, P2tog, P3. *30(32:34:36:38:40) sts.*

Working decs as set, dec 1 st at both ends of next row and every foll alt row until 12(12:14: 14:16:16) sts rem, then on foll row, so ending with RS facing for cast-off.

Cast off rem 10(10:12:12:14:14) sts.

Front

Work as given for Back until 20(20:20:22:22:22) sts rem, so ending with WS facing for next row.

P 1 row.

Shape neck

Next row (RS) K3, K2tog, K2tog tbl, K1, turn leaving rem sts unworked.

Next row P1, P2tog, P3.

Next row K1, sl 1, K2tog, psso, K1.

Next row P3tog and fasten off.

With RS facing, slip centre 4(4:4:6:6:6) sts onto a st holder, rejoin yarn and work as follows:

Next row K1, K2tog, K2tog tbl, K3.

Next row P3, P2tog tbl, P1.

Next row K1, K3tog tbl, K1.

Next row P3tog and fasten off.

Sleeves

Using 10mm (US size 15) needles and one strand of A and one strand of B held tog, cast on 24(26:28:28:30:32) sts.

Beg with a K row, work 6 rows in st st.

Change to 12mm (US size 17) needles and work as follows:

Next row (inc) K3, M1, K to last 3 sts, M1, K3.

Cont in st st throughout, inc 1 st at both ends of every foll 10th row until there are 34(36:38:38:40:42) sts.

Cont without shaping until work measures 46(46:47:47:48:48)cm/18(18:18½:18½:19:19)in from cast-on edge, ending with RS facing for next row.

Shape raglan

Cast off 3 sts at beg of next 2 rows. *28(30:32:32:34:36) sts.*

Next row (dec on RS) K3, K2tog, K to last 5 sts, K2tog tbl, K3.

Work 3 rows without shaping, so ending with RS facing for next row.

Working decs as set, dec 1 st at both ends of next row and every foll alt row until 12 sts rem, so ending with WS facing for next row.

P 1 row.

For left sleeve only

Dec 1 st at both ends of next row. *10 sts.*

Cast off 3 sts at beg of next row. *7 sts.*

Dec 1 st at beg of next row. *6 sts.*

Cast off 3 sts at beg of next row. *3 sts.*

Cast off rem 3 sts.

For right sleeve only

Cast off 4 sts at beg and dec 1 st at end of next row. *7 sts.*

P 1 row.

Cast off 3 sts at beg and dec 1 st at end of next row. *3 sts.*

P 1 row.

Cast off rem 3 sts.

Neckband

Gently steam the pieces on the reverse, but allow bottom edges of Sleeves, Back and Front to curl up onto the right side of the garment.

Join both front and back raglan seams.

With RS facing and using 12mm (US size 17) circular needle and one strand of A and one strand of B held tog, pick up and K 10(10:12:12:14:14) sts across back neck, 10 sts across left sleeve, 4 sts down right neck, K 4(4:4:6:6:6) sts from holder at front neck, pick up and K 4 sts up right neck and 10 sts across right sleeve. *42(42:44:46:48:48) sts.*

Work 3 rounds in K1, P1 rib.

Cast off in rib.

To finish

Weave in any loose yarn ends.

Join side and sleeve seams.

3 Phased Throw

The dip-dyed or phased colour effect in this simple garter-stitch throw is created by using two balls of tonal hand-dyed yarn held together as one yarn, to create beautiful subtle shades. The throw is finished at one end with a binding of soft leather.

Skill level

BEGINNER

In this project you will learn...
Plying; phasing colours

Stitches used
Garter stitch (K every row)

Materials
Double-knitting-weight hand-dyed wool yarn, such as Madeline Tosh *Tosh DK* (100% superwash merino wool; 206m/225yd per 100g/3½oz hank;  LIGHT) in the following 5 colours:
- A brown (Twig) – 2 hanks
- B bright aqua blue (Baltic) – 2 hanks
- C dark denim blue (Worn Denim) – 2 hanks
- D grey aqua (Cove) – 2 hanks
- E light green-blue (Well Water) – 2 hanks

10mm (US size 15) circular knitting needle, 100cm (40in) long
Piece of fine soft brown leather, for binding one end of throw

Note: Yarn amounts given are based on average requirements and are approximate.

Size
Approximately 122cm x 141.5cm (48¾in x 56½in)

Tension
10 sts and 14 rows to 10cm (4in) square measured over garter stitch using 10mm (US size 15) needles and two strands of yarn held together. Use larger or smaller needles if necessary to obtain the correct tension.

Abbreviations
See page 143.

Notes
Knitting in rows with a long circular needle
The throw is knitted back and forth in rows on the long circular needle to accommodate the large number of stitches.

Joining in a new colour for stripes
On the row before you need the new colour, work to the last stitch. Taking the end of the new colour, use together with the yarn in work to work the last stitch, creating a 'double stitch'. On the first stitch of next row, work the double stitch as one stitch with just the end of the new colour. This will securely 'anchor' your new yarn and neither create unsightly knots nor create bumps.

Preparing the yarn
Wind the hanks of hand-dyed yarn into balls and label each colour A, B, C, D and E.

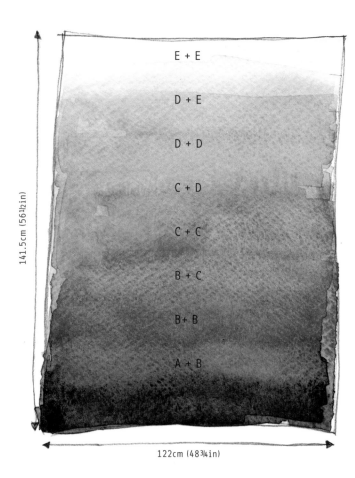

141.5cm (56½in)

122cm (48¾in)

E + E

D + E

D + D

C + D

C + C

B + C

B + B

A + B

■ A
■ B
■ C
□ D
□ E

To make the throw

Using two strands of A held together as one yarn (A+A), cast on 122 sts.

Working in garter st (K every row) throughout, work in bands of phased colour as follows:

Band 1

Cont to use A+A, work 22 rows, approximately 15cm (6in).

Band 2

Drop one strand of A and introduce one strand of B (A+B), then work 22 rows, approximately 15cm (6in).

Band 3

Drop A and introduce another strand of B (B+B), then work 22 rows, approximately 15cm (6in).

Band 4

Drop one strand of B and introduce one strand of C (B+C), then work 22 rows, approximately 15cm (6in).

Band 5

Drop B and introduce another strand of C (C+C), then work 22 rows, approximately 15cm (6in).

Band 6

Drop one strand of C and introduce an one strand of D (C+D), then work 22 rows, approximately 15cm (6in).

Band 7

Drop C and introduce another strand of D (D+D), then work 22 rows, approximately 15cm (6in).

Band 8

Drop one strand of D and introduce one strand of E (D+E), then work 22 rows, approximately 15cm (6in).

Band 9

Drop D and introduce another strand of E (E+E), then work 22 rows, approximately 15cm (6in). Cast off.

To finish

Weave in any loose yarn ends.

Cut the brown leather into narrow strips 12mm (½in) wide. Use the strips to bind the cast-on edge with overcast stitches, knotting in a new strip when necessary and leaving loose ends.

4 Primary Striped Throw

A colourful, vibrant and easy to knit 'wrap-a-round' throw is created here using a simple technique to join in new colours. It is knitted in super-chunky wool yarn and has wide crisp rib borders at the top and bottom and neat narrow rib selvedge edges.

Skill level

EASY

In this project you will learn...
Joining in new colours

Stitches used
Stocking stitch; K2, P2 rib

Materials
Super-chunky-weight wool yarn, such as Erika
   Knight *Maxi Wool* (100% British wool; 80m/87yd
   per 100g/3½oz hank; ⑥ SUPER BULKY) in the
   following 6 colours:
   A dark dusky green (Gunk 021) — 3 hanks
   B black (Pitch 025) — 2 hanks
   C off white (Canvas 001) — 1 hank
   D brown (Milk Chocolate 044) — 3 hanks
   E tomato red (Manga 047) — 1 hank
   F olive green (Artisan 020) — 2 hanks
12mm (US size 17) circular knitting needle, 100cm
   (40in) long
Large blunt-tipped sewing needle

Size
Approximately 115cm x 149cm (46in x 59½in)

Tension
8½ sts and 12 rows to 10cm (4in) square
measured over st st using 12mm (US size 17)
needles. Use smaller or larger needles if
necessary to obtain the correct tension.

Abbreviations
See page 143.

Notes
Knitting in rows with a long circular needle
The throw is knitted back and forth in rows on
the long circular needle to accommodate the
large number of stitches.

Joining in a new ball
Ensure that you have sufficient yarn to complete
a row to avoid joining in a new ball in the middle
of a row.

Joining in a new colour for stripes
On the row before you need the new colour, work
to the last stitch. Taking the end of the new
colour, use together with the yarn in work to
work the last stitch, creating a 'double stitch'. On
the first stitch of next row, work the double stitch
as one stitch with just the end of the new colour.
This will securely 'anchor' your new yarn and
neither create unsightly knots nor create bumps.

Stripe sequence
A 14 rows (in rib)
B 32 rows
C 7 rows
D 44 rows
C 4 rows
B 9 rows
C 3 rows
E 12 rows
C 3 rows
F 19 rows
C 5 rows
A 14 rows
A 14 rows (in rib)

149cm (59½in)

115cm (46in)

Using A, cast on 98 sts.
Work in rib as follows:
Row 1 (RS) [K2, P2] to last 2 sts, K2.
Row 2 P2, [K2, P2] to end of row.
Rep the last 2 rows 6 times more – this completes
the first 14 rows worked in A (as indicated in
Stripe Sequence left).
Change to B and cont in st st with rib selvedge
edges as follows:
Next row (RS) K2, P2, K to last 4 sts, P2, K2.
Next row P2, K2, P to last 4 sts, K2, P2.
Rep the last 2 rows until the 32-row stripe in B
has been completed.
Change to C and cont in st st with rib selvedge
edges as set **and at the same time** follow the
Stripe Sequence starting with the 7-row stripe in
C until the last 14-row st st stripe in A has been
completed, so ending with RS facing for next row.
Then still using A, work in rib as follows:
Row 1 (RS) (K2, P2) to last 2 sts, K2.
Row 2 P2, (K2, P2) to end of row.
Rep the last 2 rows 6 times more – this completes
the last 14 rows worked in A.
Cast off in rib.

To finish
Weave in any loose yarn ends.
Lay the work out flat and gently steam on the
reverse to enhance the yarn, avoiding the
ribbing.

5 Stripe and Print Cushion

An easy way to ensure colours work together is to take the palette from a painting, textile or ceramic. The vibrant colours of a Liberty print fabric form the basis of this contemporary cushion. The mercerised cotton yarn gives a fresh appearance and works well with the fabric back.

Skill level

◀■■□□▷
EASY

In this project you will learn...
How to change colours

Stitches used...
Stocking stitch (K 1 row, P 1 row alternately)

Materials
Fine-weight cotton yarn, such as Rowan *Cotton Glacé* (100% mercerised cotton; 115m/125yd per 50g/1¾oz ball; **2** FINE) in the following 8 colours:

    A light grey (Dawn Grey 831) – 1 ball
    B plum (Garnet 841) – 1 ball
    C mustard (Dijon 739) – 1 ball
    D turquoise (Winsor 849) – 1 ball
    E dark red (blood orange 445) – 1 ball
    F bright pink (Bubbles 724) – 1 ball
    G black (Black 727) – 1 ball
    H pale green (Shoot 814) – 1 ball
Pair of 3.75mm (US size 5) knitting needles
Large blunt-tipped sewing needle
50cm (½yd) of a cotton fabric print, for back
Sewing needle and matching sewing thread, for fabric back
Rectangular feather cushion pad, 38cm x 30cm (15in x 12in)

Note: Yarn amounts given are based on average requirements and are approximate.

Size
Approximately 38cm x 30cm (15in x 12in)

Tension
22 sts and 32 rows to 10cm (4in) square measured over st st using 3.75mm (US 5) needles. Use larger or smaller needles if necessary to obtain the correct tension.

Abbreviations
See page 143.

Note
Joining in a new colour for stripes
On the row before you need the new colour, work to the last stitch. Taking the end of the new colour, use together with the yarn in work to work the last stitch, creating a 'double stitch'. On the first stitch of next row, work the double stitch as one stitch with just the end of the new colour. This will securely 'anchor' your new yarn and neither create unsightly knots nor create bumps.

To make the cushion-cover front
Using A, cast on 66 sts.
Beg with a K row, work in st st in the following stripe sequence:
A 3 rows
B 5 rows
C 5 rows
D 3 rows
E 5 rows
C 5 rows
A 3 rows
F 7 rows
A 1 row
G 2 rows
A 5 rows
E 3 rows
H 7 rows
G 6 rows
A 3 rows
B 2 rows
C 3 rows
B 4 rows
E 4 rows
F 6 rows
A 3 rows
D 5 rows
C 3 rows
F 2 rows
A 4 rows
G 3 rows
H 4 rows
D 3 rows
B 5 rows
D 1 row
E 4 rows
A 3 rows
Cast off.

To finish the cushion-cover front
Weave in any loose yarn ends.
Lay the work out flat and gently steam on the reverse to enhance the yarn.

To add the fabric cushion-cover back
Cut a piece of fabric the same size as the knitted front plus 1.5cm (1/2in) extra all around for the seam allowance.
With right sides together, pin the cushion-cover front to the fabric along the seam lines, easing to fit. Using matching thread and a sewing needle, stitch the knitted front to the fabric back piece around three sides.
Turn the cushion cover right side out. Insert the cushion pad and sew the remaining side closed.

6 Diagonal Stripe Dishcloths

Take colour inspiration from the simplest of sources, for example, the crisp white and bold stripe linens of utilitarian tea cloths. With its narrow stripes, this traditional 'diagonal' square is knitted in garter stitch in hemp yarn, which is sustainable and naturally abrasive.

Skill level

EASY

In this project you will learn...

Joining in a new colour; using the wrong side of the stripe; increasing and decreasing

Stitches used

Garter stitch (K every row)

Materials

Double-knitting-weight hamp yarn, such as
  Lana Knits *Allhemp6* (100% hemp; 150m/165yd
  per 100g/3½oz hank; (**3**) LIGHT) in the following
  3 colours:
    A off white (Pearl 010) – 1 hank
    B red (Raspberry 011) – 1 hank
    C beige (Classic 012) – 1 hank
Pair of 3.75mm (US size 5) knitting needles
Large blunt-tipped sewing needle

Size

Approximately 25cm x 25cm (10in x 10in)

Tension

17 sts and 37 rows to 10cm (4in) square measured over garter stitch using 3.75mm (US size 5) needles. Use smaller or larger needles if necessary to obtain the correct tension.

Abbreviations

K2tog knit 2 sts together
See also page 143.

Note

Joining in a new colour for stripes
On the row before you need the new colour, work to the last stitch. Taking the end of the new colour, use together with the yarn in work to work the last stitch, creating a 'double stitch'. On the first stitch of next row, work the double stitch as one stitch with just the end of the new colour. This will securely 'anchor' your new yarn and neither create unsightly knots nor create bumps.

25cm (10in) 25cm (10in)

To make the white dishcloth with red stripes
Using A, cast on 2 sts.
Row 1 K1, K into front and back of last st (to inc 1 st). *3 sts.*
Row 2 K2, K into front and back of last st. *4 sts.*
Row 3 K to last st, K into front and back of last st. *5 sts.*
Rep row 3 until there are 62 sts on needle.
Next row K.
Next row (dec) K to last 2 sts, K2tog (to dec 1 st). *61 sts.*
Rep last row until 43 sts rem.
Cont to dec as set **and at the same time** work stripes as follows:
B 2 rows
A 3 rows
B 4 rows
A 3 rows
B 2 rows
Using A, cont to dec as set until 2 sts rem.
Next row K2tog and fasten off.

To make the white dishcloth with beige and red stripes
Using A, cast on 2 sts.
Row 1 K1, K into front and back of last st (to inc 1 st). *3 sts.*
Row 2 K2, K into front and back of last st. *4 sts.*
Row 3 K to last st, K into front and back of last st. *5 sts.*
Rep row 3 until there are 19 sts on needle.
Cont to inc as set, work 4 rows in C.
Using A, cont to inc as set until there are 62 sts on needle.
Next row K.
Next row (dec) K to last 2 sets, K2tog (to dec 1 st). *61 sts.*
Rep last row until 53 sts rem.
Cont to dec as set **and at the same time** work stripes as follows:
C 4 rows
A 2 rows
B 2 rows
A 2 rows
B 2 rows
A 2 rows
C 4 rows
Using A, cont to dec as set until 2 sts rem.
Next row K2tog and fasten off.

To finish both dishcloths
Weave in any loose yarn ends.
Lay the work out flat and gently steam on the reverse to enhance the yarn.

7 Patterned Pouffe

Here's a quick and fun lesson in striping, to make a practical pouffe. Rib stitch stripes create an energetic 'broken' pattern and a vibrant textile, which is perfect for this colourful pouffe where a tight fit over the inner beanbag is required.

Skill level

EASY

In this project you will learn...
How to change colour; working even- and odd-row stripes

Stitches used
K1, P1 rib; K1, P2 rib

Materials
Super-chunky-weight wool yarn, such as Erika
   Knight *Maxi Wool* (100% British wool; 80m/87yd
   per 100g/3½oz hank; (6) SUPER BULKY) in the
   following 8 colours:
   A pale grey (Flax 002) – 2 hanks
   B black (Pitch 025) – 1 hanks
   C aqua blue (Mallard 031) – 1 hank
   D burgundy red (House Red 046) – 1 hank
   E light blue (Steve 032) – 1 hank
   F medium grey (Storm 004) – 1 hank
   G steel blue (Classic 038) – 1 hank
   H bright red (Marni 030) – 1 hank
9mm (US size 13) circular knitting needle, 100cm
   (40in) long
Inexpensive beanbag (or duvet or polystyrene
   beads in a fabric bag)

Note: Yarn amounts given are based on average requirements and are approximate.

Size
Finished pouffe is approximately 39cm (15½in) high and 165cm (65in) in circumference

Tension
10 sts and 14 rows to 10cm (4in) square measured over rib patt using 9mm (US size 13) needles. Use smaller or larger needles if necessary to obtain the correct tension.

Abbreviations
K3tog tbl knit 3 sts together through back loops
P2tog purl 2 sts together
See also page 143.

Notes
Knitting in rows with a long circular needle
The pouffe cover is knitted back and forth in rows on the long circular needle to accommodate the large number of stitches.

Joining in a new colour for stripes
On the row before you need the new colour, work to the last stitch. Taking the end of the new colour, use together with the yarn in work to work the last stitch, creating a 'double stitch'. On the first stitch of next row, work the double stitch as one stitch with just the end of the new colour. This will securely 'anchor' your new yarn and neither create unsightly knots nor create bumps.

Stripe sequence

*B 5 rows
C 1 row
A 2 rows
B 1 row
D 4 rows on first rep; H 4 rows on second rep
E 1 row
F 3 rows
B 2 rows
C 6 rows
B 1 row
E 1 row
G 1 row
E 1 row
A 1 row
F 1 row
A 1 row
C 1 row
A 4 rows
D 1 row on first rep; H 1 row on second rep
A 2 rows
F 1 row
G 8 rows
A 1 row
Repeat sequence starting from *.

To make the pouffe cover

Using B, cast on 34 sts.
Row 1 K.
Row 2 [K into front and back in each st] to last st, K1. *67 sts.*
Row 3 K.
Row 4 [K into front and back in each st] to end of row. *134 sts.*
Keeping Stripe Sequence correct (see left), cont in rib as follows:
Row 1 (RS) Using B, [P2, K1] to last 2 sts, P2.
Row 2 Using C, [K2, P1] to last 2 sts, K2.
Starting with first 2-row stripe in A, cont in Stripe Sequence throughout **and at the same time** rep last 2 rows until 88 rows have been worked from cast-on edge and work measures approximately 63cm (25in), ending with RS facing for next row.
Keeping Stripe Sequence correct dec as follows:
Row 1 (RS) [P2tog, K1] to last 2 sts, P2tog. *89 sts.*
Row 2 [K1, P1] to last st, K1.
Row 3 [P1, K3tog tbl] to last st, P1. *45 sts.*
Row 4 [K1, P1] to last st, K1.
Row 5 [P1, K3tog tbl] to last st, P1. *23 sts.*
Cut yarn, leaving a long end.
Thread yarn end through rem sts, pull up tightly and fasten securely. Don't cut the yarn but use it to sew side seam, stopping about 30cm (12in) from the cast-on edge.

To finish

Insert the beanbag inners.
Finish sewing side seam and fasten securely.
Thread yarn through the cast-on edge, pull up tightly and fasten securely.

8 Boot Toppers

This slip-stitch colour pattern creates a great textile on each side, so it's a difficult choice which to use. It has quite a retro 'Fair Isle' appearance so is certain to be a firm favourite. These simple boot toppers are a great project to try in this stitch.

Skill level

EASY

In this project you will learn...
How to work a slip-stitch colour pattern

Stitches used
Stocking stitch slip-stitch colour pattern;
K1, P1 rib

Materials
Aran-weight wool yarn, such as Erika Knight
  Vintage Wool (100% pure British wool;
  87m/95yd per 50g/1¾oz hank; (4) MEDIUM) in
  the following 7 colours:
    A light grey (Drizzle) – 1 hank
    B dark grape (Mulberry) – 1 hank
    C light blue (Steve) – 1 hank
    D dark blue (Dark) – 1 hank
    E fuchsia (Gorgeous) – 1 hank
    F light brown (Bambi) – 1 hank
    G pale beige (Flax) – 1 hank
Pair of 5mm (US size 8) knitting needles
Large blunt-tipped sewing needle

Note: Yarn amounts given are based on average requirements and are approximate.

Size
One size
Approximately 36cm (14¼in) in circumference around slip-stitch pattern, unstretched

Tension
18 sts and 24 rows to 10cm (4in) square measured over st st using 5mm (US size 8) needles. Use larger or smaller needles if necessary to obtain the correct tension.

Abbreviations
See page 143.

Note
Working the slip-stitch colour pattern
Only one colour is used in each row of the slip-stitch colour pattern. When slipping stitches on right-side rows hold the yarn at the back of the work and when slipping stitches on a wrong-side row hold the yarn at the front of the work. All slip stitches are slipped purlwise, inserting the needle into the stitches you are slipping as if to purl (see page 36).

To make the boot toppers
Using A, cast on 74 sts.
Row 1 (RS) Using A, K.
Row 2 Using A, P.
Row 3 Using B, K2, *sl 4, K2; rep from * to end.
Row 4 Using B, P3, sl 2, *P4, sl 2; rep from * to last 3 sts, P3.
Rows 5 Using B, K.
Row 6 Using B, P.
Row 7 Using C, K1, sl 2, K2, *sl 4, K2; rep from * to last 3 sts, sl 2, K1.
Row 8 Using C, P1, sl 1, P4, *sl 2, P4; rep from * to last 2 sts, sl 1, P1.
Rows 9 Using C, K.
Row 10 Using C, P.
Rows 11 Using D, K2, *sl 4, K2; rep from * to end.
Row 12 Using D, P3, sl 2, *P4, sl 2; rep from * to last 3 sts, P3.
Rows 13 Using D, K.
Row 14 Using D, P.
Rows 15 Using E, K1, sl 2, K2, *sl 4, K2; rep from * to last 3 sts, sl 2, K1.
Row 16 Using E, P1, sl 1, P4, *sl 2, P4; rep from * to last 2 sts, sl 1, P1.
Row 17 Using E, K.
Row 18 Using E, P.
Row 19 Using B, K2, *sl 4, K2; rep from * to end.
Row 20 Using B, P3, sl 2, *P4, sl 2; rep from * to last 3 sts, P3.
Row 21 Using B, K.
Row 22 Using B, P.
Row 23 Using F, K1, sl 2, K2, *sl 4, K2; rep from * to last 3 sts, sl 2, K1.
Row 24 Using F, P1, sl 1, P4, *sl 2, P4; rep from * to last 2 sts, sl 1, P1.
Row 25 Using F, K.

Row 26 Using F, P.
Row 27 Using G, K2, *sl 4, K2; rep from * to end.
Row 28 Using G, P3, sl 2, *P4, sl 2; rep from * to last 3 sts, P3.
Row 29 Using G, K.
Row 30 Using G, P.
Row 31 Using D, K1, sl 2, K2, *sl 4, K2; rep from * to last 3 sts, sl 2, K1.
Row 32 Using D, P1, sl 1, P4, *sl 2, P4; rep from * to last 2 sts, sl 1, P1.

Cont in K1, P1 rib as follows:
D 2 rows
B 1 row
A 4 rows
E 1 row
D 3 rows
B 2 rows
C 6 rows
B 1 row
E 1 row
F 1 row
E 1 row
G 1 row
D 1 row
G 1 row
C 1 row
G 2 rows
Cast off in rib.

To finish
Weave in any loose yarn ends.
Lay the work out flat and gently steam on the reverse to enhance the yarn, avoiding the ribbing.
Sew the side seam.

9 Tweed Stitch Muffler Scarf

The colours of men's silk foulard patterns and quintessential British tweeds are the inspiration for this simple 'tweed' stitch muffler. Worked in three colours in soft linen for drape, stitch clarity and richness of tones, it also has a contrasting teal cast-off edge.

Skill level...

EASY

In this project you will learn...
How to work a slip-stitch colour pattern

Stitches used...
Slip-stitch colour pattern

Materials
Double-knitting-weight linen-cotton yarn, such as Rowan *Creative Linen* (50% linen, 50% cotton; 200m/219yd per 100g/3½oz hank; (3) LIGHT) in the following 4 colours:
   A dark steel blue (Stormy 635) – 1 hank
   B maroon red (Coleus 637) – 1 hank
   C light green (Apple 629) – 1 hank
   D light teal blue (Teal 625) – 1 hank
Pair of 5mm (US size 8) knitting needles
Large blunt-tipped sewing needle

Size
Approximately 17.5cm x 102cm (7in x 40½in)

Tension
26 sts and 34 rows to 10cm (4in) square measured over pattern using 5mm (US size 8) needles. Use larger or smaller needles if necessary to obtain the correct tension.

Abbreviations
See page 143.

Note
Working the slip-stitch colour pattern
Only one colour is used in each row of the slip-stitch pattern. All slip stitches are slipped purlwise, inserting the needle into the stitches you are slipping as if to purl (see page 36).

To make the scarf
Using A, cast on 45 sts.
Set-up row (WS) Using A, P.
Row 1 (RS) Using B, K1, *yf, sl 1, yb, K1; rep from * to end.
Row 2 Using C, K1, P1, * yb, sl 1, yf, P1; rep from * to last st, K1.
Row 3 Using A, rep row 1.
Row 4 Using B, rep row 2.
Row 5 Using C, rep row 1.
Row 6 Using A, rep row 2.
Rep last 6 rows until work measures 100cm (39½in) from cast-on edge, ending with RS facing for next row.
Change to D and work 4 rows in patt.
Cast off in patt using D.

To finish
Weave in any loose yarn ends.
Lay the work out flat and gently steam on the reverse to enhance the yarn.

10 Fair Isle Snood

The 'stranding' on the inside of the knitting on this simple Fair Isle pattern in classic black and white creates a 'woven fabric' effect — always a favourite of mine when allowed to show. The cast-on and cast-off rows are each worked in a contrasting colour to accentuate this effect.

Skill level

■ ■ ■ ◗

EXPERIENCED

In this project you will learn...

Working in the round; working with two colours in a round using the stranding technique

Stitches used

Knit

Materials

Aran-weight wool yarn, such as Erika Knight *Vintage Wool* (100% pure British wool; 87m/95yd per 50g/1¾oz hank; **4** MEDIUM) in the following 4 colours:

    A pale beige (Flax) – 3 hanks
    B black (Pitch) – 2 hanks
    C fuchsia (Gorgeous) – small amount
    D aqua (Leighton) – small amount
5mm (US size 8) circular knitting needle, 75cm (30in) long
Large blunt-tipped sewing needle

Size

Approximately 100cm x 32cm (40in x 12¾in)

Tension

18 sts and 21 rows to 10cm (4in) square measured over Fair Isle pattern using 5mm (US size 8) needles. Use larger or smaller needles if necessary to obtain the correct tension.

Abbreviations

See page 143.

Notes

Working the pattern in rounds from the chart
When working the stocking stitch Fair Isle pattern in rounds on the circular needle note that every stitch is a knit stitch, and read all rows of the chart from right to left.

Stranding
Work the Fair Isle pattern using the stranding technique. No more that two colours are used in a row, and the colour not in use is stranded at the back of the knitting (see pages 28–31).

To make the snood

Using 5mm (US size 8) circular needle and C, cast on 180 sts.
Place a st marker on tip of right needle to mark start of round, then K 1 round.
Change to yarn A and using the stranding technique, work chart rounds 2–66 in st st (knit every round), changing colour where indicated, reading all rows from right to left and working the 36-st chart repeat 5 times for each round.
Using D, K 1 round (chart round 67).
Cast off in D.

To finish

Weave in any loose yarn ends.
Lay the work out flat and gently steam on the reverse to enhance the yarn.

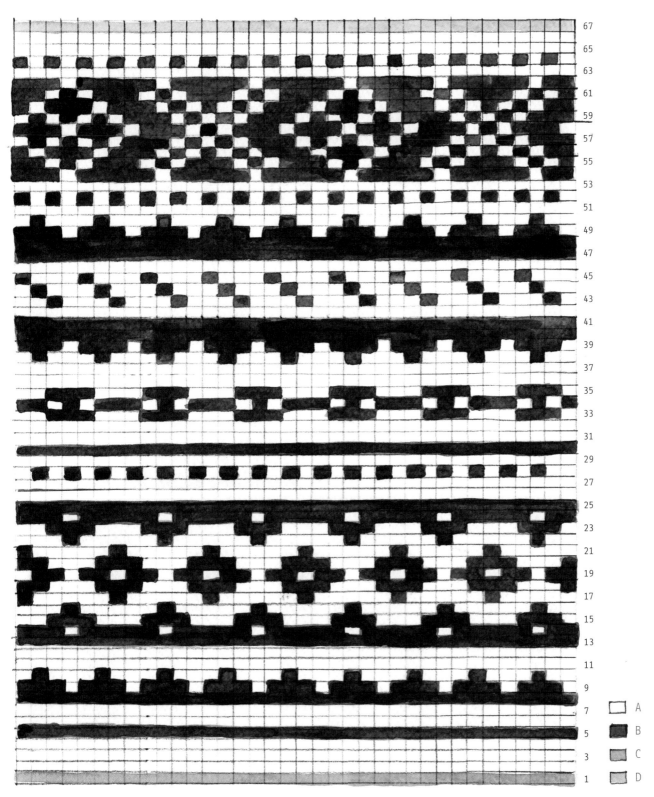

67
65
63
61
59
57
55
53
51
49
47
45
43
41
39
37
35
33
31
29
27
25
23
21
19
17
15
13
11
9
7
5
3
1

☐ A
■ B
▨ C
▢ D

patt repeat = 36 sts (entire width of chart)

11 Houndstooth Hat

This basic beanie shaped hat has a rolled edge at the brim. It is knitted in a two-colour houndstooth pattern using the simple 'stranding' technique and is topped off with a huge impressive two-colour pompom.

Skill level

EXPERIENCED

In this project you will learn...

How to knit a pattern with two colours in a row using the stranding technique; how to make a pompom

Stitches used

Stocking stitch

Materials

Super-chunky-weight wool yarn, such as Erika
   Knight *Maxi Wool* (100% British wool; 80m/87yd
   per 100g/3½oz hank; **6** SUPER BULKY) in the
   following 2 colours:
   For the green and black version
      A olive green (Artisan 020) – 1 hank
      B black (Pitch 025) – 1 hank
   For the tomato red and black version
      A tomato red (Manga 214) – 1 hank
      B black (Pitch 025) – 1 hank
Pair of 12mm (US size 17) knitting needles
Large blunt-tipped sewing needle
Piece of stiff cardboard, for making pompom

Note: Yarn amounts given are based on average requirements and are approximate.

Size

One size to fit average adult head
Approximately 51cm (20½in) in circumference, unstretched

Tension

10 sts and 10½ rows measured over 10cm (4in) square over colour pattern with 12mm (US size 17) needles. Use larger or smaller needles if necessary to obtain the correct tension.

Abbreviations

K2tog knit 2 sts together
See also page 143.

Notes

Working the pattern from the chart
When working the stocking stitch houndstooth pattern in rows, read all knit (odd-numbered) rows from right to left and all purl (even-numbered) rows from left to right.

Stranding
Work the houndstooth pattern using the stranding technique. Two colours are used in a row, and the colour not in use is stranded at the back of the knitting (see pages 28–31).

To make the hat

Using B, cast on 51 sts.

Beg with a K row, work in st st houndstooth pattern from chart using the stranding technique as follows:

Row 1 (RS) Following 10-st chart pattern repeat from right to left, work [K1B, K7A, K2B] 5 times, then work first st of pattern repeat once more (that is, K1B).

Row 2 Work last st (at right of chart) of pattern repeat (that is, P1B), then following 10-st chart pattern repeat from left to right, work [P1B, P8A, P1B] 5 times.

These 2 rows set chart placement.

Cont in patt, working 14-row repeat as set on chart once, then rows 1–10 once more, so ending with RS facing for next row.

Using A only, cont as follows:

Next row [Sl 1, K2tog, psso] 17 times. *17 sts.*

Cut yarn leaving a long end, thread end through remaining sts, pull up tightly and fasten securely.

To finish

Sew the hat seam.

Weave in any loose yarns ends.

Gently steam the work on the reverse to enhance the yarn.

To make the pompom

Cut out two cardboard circles approximately 13cm (5in) in diameter and cut an identical hole in the centre of each one.

Hold the circles together and using B wound into a ball small enough to pass through the centre of the hole, wind the yarn over the circles, keeping the strands close together. Add a layer of A in the same way. Alternating B and A, work as many layers as you can before the centre of the hole becomes too small for a ball to pass through.

Using sharp scissors, slip one of the blades between the two layers of cardboard and cut around the circle and through the yarn.

Wrap a length of yarn tightly around the centre off the pompom between the two cardboard circles and knot the yarn securely, leaving long ends to secure the pompom to the hat. Cut away the cardboard.

Then shake, fluff and trim the pompom and sew it to the top of the hat.

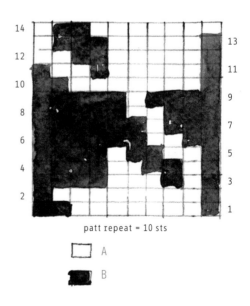

patt repeat = 10 sts

☐ A

■ B

12 Scandi Socks

These Fair Isle pattern slouchy socks are worked with five double-pointed needles. The pattern is knitted using the stranding technique and looks great in two or even three colours. Alternatively work each pattern section in different colours for a really personal effect.

Skill level

EXPERIENCED

In this project you will learn...

Working in the round; working with two colours in a round using the stranding technique (see pages 28–30)

Stitches used

Knit

Materials

Double-knitting-weight wool yarn, such as Erika Knight *British Blue Wool* (100% Blue-Faced Leicester wool; 55m/60yd per 25g/¾oz ball; **3** LIGHT) in the following 2 colours:
  A grey (Mouse 039) – 3 balls
  B pale gold (Gift 040) – 3 balls
Set of five 3.75mm (US size 5) double-pointed knitting needles
Set of five 4mm (US size 6) double-pointed knitting needles
Large blunt-tipped sewing needle

Note: Yarn amounts given are based on average requirements and are approximate.

Size

To fit an average woman's foot, length 20–25cm (8–10in)

Knitted measurements (unstretched)

Foot circumference 20cm (8in)
Leg circumference 25cm (10in)
Length from sole 30cm (12in)

Tension

24 sts and 27 rows to 10cm (4in) square measured over colour pattern using 4mm (US size 6) needles. Use larger or smaller needles if necessary to obtain the correct tension.

Abbreviations

See page 143.

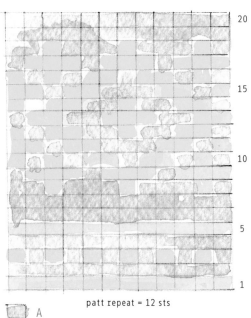

patt repeat = 12 sts

 A

 B

To make the left sock

Using 3.75mm (US size 5) double-pointed needles and B, cast on 60 sts, distributing them evenly over four needles.

Place a marker to mark beg of round and join to work in the round, taking care not to twist sts and using fifth needle to knit with.

K 18 rounds, ending at marker.

Change to A and K 12 rounds, ending at marker.

Fold up hem

Next round K the first st of round tog with corresponding loop from cast-on edge, then rep this process with each st and its corresponding cast-on loop to end of round.

Change to 4mm (US size 6) needles and using A, K 2 rounds.

Begin chart

[Knitting every round, work chart rounds 1–20] twice, repeating 12-st patt repeat 5 times in each round and using the stranding technique.

Rep chart rounds 1–6 once more.

Cont in A only, K 2 rounds.

Next round *K3, K2tog; rep from * to end. *48 sts.*

K 2 rounds.**

Place sts for heel

Cut yarn and slip first 24 sts purlwise without working them.

With a strand of contrasting waste yarn about 60cm (24in) long, K 24 sts and slip next 24 sts.

Rejoin A and K the 24 sts worked in waste yarn, then K to end of round.

Place marker to mark beg of round.

Using A, K 3 rounds, making first and last sts slightly tighter to prevent holes.

Begin chart

Work chart rounds 1–20, repeating 12-st patt repeat 4 times in each round; then rep chart rounds 1–7 once more.

Using A, K 2 rounds.

Work toe

Change to 3.75mm (US size 3) needles and B.

Decrease round 1 *K1, K2tog tbl, K18, K2tog, K1*, place marker; rep from * to * once more.

Note: The two markers mark the positions of the decreases.

K 2 rounds without shaping.

Decrease round 2 *K1, K2tog tbl, K to 3 sts before marker, K2tog, K1*; rep from * to * once more.

K 1 round without shaping.

Rep last 2 rounds twice more.

Cont to work *decrease round 2* on every foll round until 8 sts rem.

K2, and split the sts over 2 needles from back to front, so there are now 2 sts from the instep and 2 sts from the sole on each of the two needles.

Cut yarn, leaving a 13cm (5in) tail, and graft sts together using Kitchener stitch.

Work heel

Remove waste yarn at heel and pick up the live sts on each side of the opening. Using 4mm (US size 6) double-pointed needles, distribute the sts evenly over the needles, so the 24 sts for the top of the heel are on two needles and the bottom 24 sts are on the other two needles. Place markers at each side of the heel opening where you will be making the decreases.

Note: Sometimes it helps to pick up an extra 2 sts either side of each marker to reduce the appearance of holes. If you decide to do this, work one extra decrease.

Change to 3.75mm (US size 5) needles and B.

Round 1 *K1, K2tog tbl, K to 3 sts before marker, K2tog, K1; rep from * once more.

Round 2 K.

Rep rounds 1 and 2 until 16 sts rem.

Distribute sts evenly over 2 needles, and graft together using Kitchener stitch.

To make the right sock

Work as for Left sock to **.

Using contrasting waste yarn, K24.

Slip next 24 sts and place marker to marker beg of round.

Pick up A and knit the 24 sts worked in waste yarn, then K to end of round.

Using A, K 3 rounds, making first and last sts slightly tighter to prevent holes.

Complete as given for Left Sock.

To finish

Weave in any loose yarn ends.

Gently steam the socks on the reverse to enhance the yarn.

13 Fanø Mittens

Influences from traditional Scandinavian designs and especially from the beautiful Danish island of Fanø are mixed up here in these fingerless mittens. They are worked in four colours with a beautiful super-fine wool-alpaca yarn on two needles.

Skill level

■■■■ ▭

EXPERIENCED

In this project you will learn...
Working with two colours in a row using the stranding technique (see pages 28–30); working from a chart

Stitches used
Stocking stitch

Materials
Super-fine-weight wool-alpaca yarn, such as
  Isager *Alpaca 2* (50% merino lambswool,
  50% baby alpaca; 247m/270yd per 50g/1¾oz
  hank; (**1**) SUPER FINE) in the following 4 colours:
    A raspberry (shade 17) – 1 hank
    B dark blue grey (shade 47) – 1 hank
    C pale blue (shade 4s) – 1 hank
    D dusky plum (shade 52) – 1 hank
Pair of 3mm (US size 3) knitting needles
Large blunt-tipped sewing needle

Size
One size to fit average woman's hand
Length from cuff edge to top edge 22cm (8¾in)

Tension
38 sts and 36 rows to 10cm (4in) square measured over colour pattern using 3mm (US size 3) needles. Use smaller or larger needles if necessary to obtain the correct tension.

Abbreviations
Pm place marker (loop a piece of contrasting yarn, or a stitch marker, onto the needle or ends of row)
See also page 143.

Notes
Working the left and right mittens
Instructions are given for the left mitten. Instructions for right mitten are in brackets.

Working from the charts
When working the stocking stitch colour pattern from the charts using the stranding technique, read the right-side (knit) rows from right to left and the wrong-side (purl) rows from left to right.

To make the mittens
Using A, cast on 70(70) sts.
Change to B and C and beg working in st st throughout as follows:
Row 1 (RS) *K1B, K1C; rep from * to end of row.
Row 2 *P1C, P1B; rep from * to end of row.
Rep last 2 rows until work measures 6.5cm (2½in) from cast-on edge, ending with RS facing for next row.
Change to D and work 2 rows st st.
Change to A and B and work chequerboard patt in st st as follows:
Next row (RS) *K1A, K1B; rep from * to end of row.
Next row *P1A, P1B; rep from * to end of row.
Rep last 2 rows 3 times more, so ending with RS facing for next row. *8 rows worked in total in chequerboard patt.*
Change to D and work 2 rows in st st, so ending with RS facing for next row.
Shape thumb gusset
Using B and C, beg working the st st colour pattern from the flower and plaid charts and start the gusset for the left(right) mitten as follows:
Row 1 (RS) K last 0(2) sts of row 1 of plaid chart, then K first 28(35) sts of row 1 of plaid(flower) chart; pm, K1B, M1, K1B, K1C, K1B, M1, K1B, pm (row 1 of thumb gusset); K last 2(0) sts of row 1 of plaid chart, then K first 35 (28) sts of row 1 of flower(plaid) chart.
Row 2 P first 35 (last 28) sts of row 2 of flower (plaid) chart, P first 2(0) sts of row 2 of plaid chart; slip marker onto right needle, P2B, P1C, P1B, P1C, P2B (row 2 of thumb gusset), slip second marker onto right needle; P last 28 (first 35) sts of row 2 of plaid(flower) chart.

The last 2 rows set the positions of the charts and the chequerboard thumb gusset.
Cont as set in chart patterns until chart row 18 has been completed **and at the same time** inc one st at each side of thumb gusset (as set in row 1) on third row and every foll alt row until there are 21 gusset sts between the markers (keeping chequerboard patt correct), ending with RS facing for next row. *86 sts.*
Work top of thumb
Row 19 (RS) Patt to the second marker, remove marker, TURN and cast on 3 sts, work in chequerboard patt to rem marker, remove marker, TURN and cast on 3 sts. *27 sts for thumb.*
Work 7 rows more in chequerboard patt on these 27 sts, so ending with WS facing for next row.
Change to A.
Next row P.
Cast off using A.
Join thumb seam using mattress st.
With RS facing, rejoin C at base of thumb and pick up and K 5 sts from base of thumb, then patt to end of row 19. *70 sts.*
Now working all sts in patt, cont until row 36 of chart has been completed, so ending with RS facing for next row.
Change to D and work 2 rows in st st.
Change to B and work 4 rows in st st.
Change to A and work 2 rows in st st.
Cast off using A.

To finish
Weave in any loose yarn ends.
Gently steam the mitterns on the reverse to enhance the yarn.
Sew the side seams using mattress stitch.

Flower chart

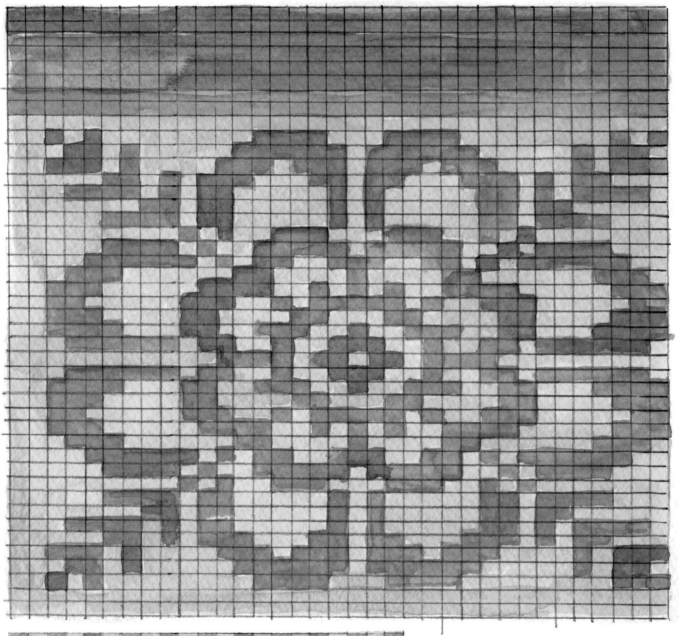

Gusset chart

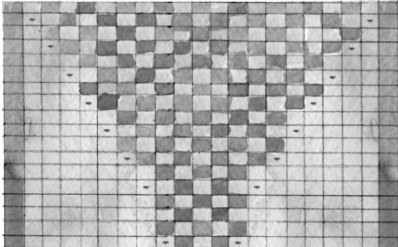

Note *Not all the squares on the gusset chart represent stitches, so follow the instructions on page 109 for shaping the gusset, referring to the chart for the positioning of the chequerboard pattern only. Note that the first and last stitch of the gusset on all rows is worked in B.*

Plaid chart

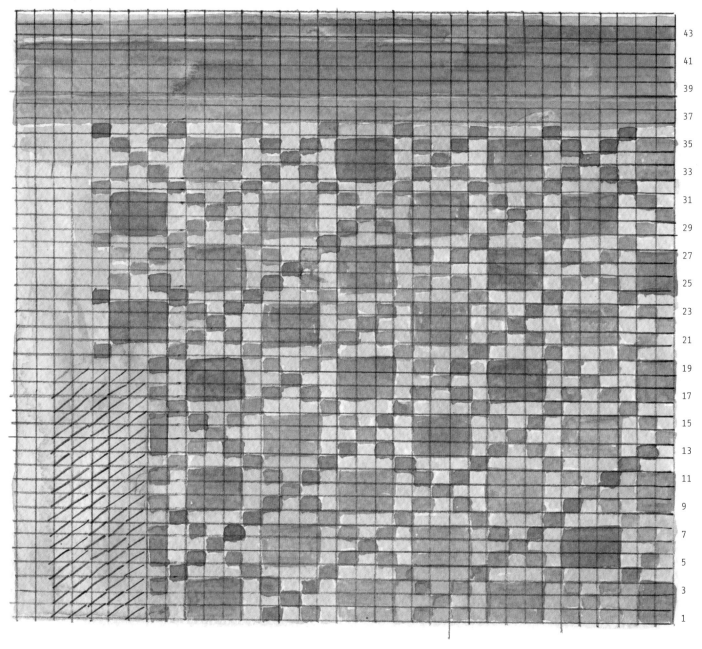

43
41
39
37
35
33
31
29
27
25
23
21
19
17
15
13
11
9
7
5
3
1

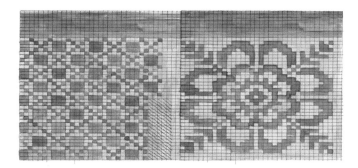

Positions of charts on right mitten

A	
B	
C	
gusset position	
increases on gusset	
D	

14 Colour Wheel Cushion

A little parody of the ubiquitous colour wheel found in every colour theory book, this round cushion is worked in stocking stitch in a linen-cotton yarn. The shape is created by the clever, simple short-row shaping technique.

Skill level

■■□□
EASY

In this project you will learn...
Simple colour blocking; short-row shaping

Stitches used
Stocking stitch

Materials
Double-knitting-weight linen-cotton yarn, such as
  Rowan *Creative Linen* (50% linen, 50% cotton;
  200m/219yd per 100g/3½oz hank; **3** LIGHT)
  in the following 8 colours:
    A dark maroon (Eggplant 638) – 1 hank
    B maroon red (Coleus 637) – 1 hank
    C pale brown (Beige 622) – 1 hank
    D light green (Apple 629) – 1 hank
    E olive green (Leaf 632) – 1 hank
    F light teal blue (Teal 625) – 1 hank
    G light denim blue (Denim 630) – 1 hank
    H dark steel blue (Stormy 635) – 1 hank
Pair of 4.5mm (US size 7) knitting needles
Large blunt-tipped sewing needle
Round feather cushion pad, approximately 40cm
  (16in) in diameter to fit finished cover

Size
Approximately 40cm (16in) in diameter

Tension
21 sts and 30 rows to 10cm (4in) square measured over st st using 4.5mm (US size 7) needles. Use smaller or larger needles as necessary to obtain the correct the tension.

Abbreviations
See page 143.

Note
Short-row shaping
For the short-row shaping, when the instructions say 'TURN' at the end of the row, this means that the remaining stitches are not worked. To avoid creating a hole when turning on a knit row, work a wrap stitch – knit as far as instructed, then slip the next stitch purlwise onto the right-hand needle, bring the yarn forward between the two needles, slip the stitch back to the left-hand needle and take the yarn to the back between the two needles, turn, and purl to the end of the next row as instructed.

Colour sequence for cushion-cover top

A
B
C
D
E
F
G
H

Colour sequence for cushion-cover base

H
G
F
E
D
C
B
A

To make the cushion-cover top

Using A, cast on 42 sts.

**Work in st st and short rows as follows:
Row 1 K.
Row 2 P.
Row 3 K to last 2 sts, turn (see Note on page 112 on how to 'turn' in short-row shaping).
Row 4 P.
Row 5 K to last 4 sts, turn.
Row 6 P.

Continue working in short rows as set, leaving 2 stitches more unworked on every knit row until there are no more stitches to knit.**
This completes the first colour segment of the circle.
Change to B and rep from ** to ** for next colour segment.
Continue repeating from ** to ** for each colour segment until 8 segments have been worked to form a full circle, following the colour sequence for the cushion-cover top.
Do not cast off stitches, but join last segment to first segment by grafting one stitch from needle with corresponding stitch on cast-on edge.

To make the cushion-cover base

Work as given for cushion-cover top, but cast on with H and use colour sequence for the cushion-cover base.

To finish

Weave in any loose yarn ends.
Lay the work out flat and gently steam on the reverse to enhance the yarn.
Using a length of yarn and a blunt-tipped sewing needle, gently gather together the small hole in the centre of each piece and fasten securely.
Sew the top and base pieces together, matching the colours along the seam and leaving an opening for inserting the cushion pad. Insert the cushion pad and sew the opening closed.

15 Geometric Patchwork Throw

Knitted using the simple colour block technique, this strong graphic patchwork-effect throw has unfinished cast-on, cast-off and side edges for a contemporary detail. It is made in a luxuriously soft merino and mohair blend for ultimate cosiness.

Skill level

INTERMEDIATE

In this project you will learn...
Colour blocking (intarsia) technique (see page 32)

Stitches used...
Stocking stitch

Materials
Chunky-weight wool-mohair yarn, such as Rowan
  Cocoon (80% merino wool, 20% kid mohair;
  115m/126yd per 100g/3¹/₂oz ball;  BULKY)
  in the following 5 colours:
    A blue-green (Seascape 813) – 3 balls
    B charcoal (Mountain 805) – 3 balls
    C medium grey (Shale 804) – 3 balls
    D light grey (Scree 803) – 3 balls
    E pale grey (Alpine 802) – 3 balls
7mm (US size 10¹/₂) circular knitting needle,
  100cm (40in) long and with a wire strong
  enough to take the weight of the project
Large blunt-tipped sewing needle

Size
Approximately 120cm x 162.5cm (48in x 65in)

Tension
14 sts and 16 rows to 10cm (4in) square measured over st st using 7mm (US size 10¹/₂) needles. Use larger or smaller needles if necessary to obtain the correct tension.

Abbreviations
See page 143.

Note
Working the colour pattern
Work each triangle with a separate small ball of yarn, and when changing colours twist the yarns at back of work to avoid a hole.

To make the throw
Using the knit cast-on, cast on 168 sts, joining in colours as follows – 27D, 1B, 1D, 27C, 27A, 1E, 1B, 27C, 27A, 1D, 1C, 27E.

Rectangles row 1
With same side of work still facing, beg patt as follows:
Row 1 (RS) K across row, using colours for the triangles with right-leaning and left-leaning diagonals in chart row 1 as follows – 27E, 1C, 1D, 27A, 27C, 1B, 1E, 27A, 27C, 1D, 1B, 27D.
Row 2 (WS) P across row, using colours for chart row 2 as follows – 26D, 2B, 2D, 26C, 26A, 2E, 2B, 26C, 26A, 2D, 2C, 26E.
This sets the positions of the first row of two-colour rectangles.
Cont in st st colour patt as set until chart row 52 has been completed, so ending with RS facing for next row.

Rectangles rows 2–5
Work rectangles rows 2–5 following the colour sequences diagram and the colour chart, ending with chart row 51 on the last row of rectangles. Cast off purlwise, using the colours as set on chart row 52.

To finish
Weave in any loose yarn ends.
Gently steam on the reverse to enhance the yarn.

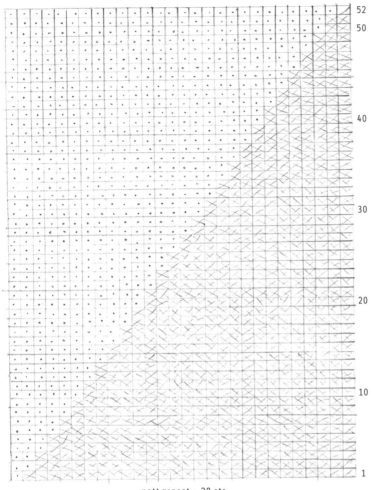

52
50

⊡ triangle one
⊠ triangle two

40

Note The chart shows the 26-st rectangle with the right-leaning diagonal; for this rectangle, read the right-side (knit) rows from right to left and the wrong-side (purl) rows from left to right. For the rectangles with the left-leaning diagonal, the chart is flopped horizontally, so to do this read the right-side (knit) rows from left to right and the wrong-side (purl) rows from right to left.

30

Colour Sequences

The colour sequences for each row of two-colour 28-st rectangles are given below from left to right, but remember that when knitting the first row of each row of rectangles, you will be introducing the colours from right to left.

20

A blue-green
B charcoal
C medium grey
D light grey
E pale grey

10

1

patt repeat = 28 sts

Rectangles row 5 C/A, E/A, D/C, A/B, A/D, E/B

Rectangles row 4 E/C, A/B, E/D, A/E, C/A, B/C

Rectangles row 3 B/D, E/C, B/A, C/A, B/D, E/A

Rectangles row 2 A/C, E/A, C/D, A/D, C/E, B/D

Rectangles row 1 D/B, D/C, A/E, B/C, A/D, C/E

16 Squares Cushion

Backed with a printed cotton fabric, this cushion has a simple squares within squares colour pattern made with the colour-block (intarsia) technique. Play with tonal colours or experiment with opposites to create a personal statement.

Skill level

◼◼◼◻

INTERMEDIATE

In this project you will learn...
Colour-blocking (intarsia) technique (see page 32); reading from a chart

Stitches used...
Stocking stitch

Materials
Double-knitting-weight wool yarn, such as Erika Knight *British Blue Wool* (100% Blue-Faced Leicester wool; 55m/60yd per 25g/¾oz ball; (**3**) LIGHT) in the following 6 colours:
  A pink (Boho 048) – 1 ball
  B pale beige (Fawn 037) – 2 balls
  C purple (French 043) – 2 balls
  D grey (Mouse 039) – 1 ball
  E brown (Milk Chocolate 044) – 1 ball
  F light blue (Iced Gem 041) – 1 ball
Pair of 3.75mm (US size 5) knitting needles
Large blunt-tipped sewing needle
50cm (½yd) of a cotton fabric print, for back
Sewing needle and matching sewing thread, for fabric back
Square feather cushion pad, 40cm x 40cm (16in x 16in)

Note: Yarn amounts given are based on average requirements and are approximate.

Size
Approximately 40cm x 40cm (16in x 16in)

Tension
22 sts and 30 rows to 10cm (4in) square measured over st st using 3.75mm (US size 5) needles. Use larger or smaller needles if necessary to obtain the correct tension.

Abbreviations
See page 143.

Notes
Working the colour pattern
Using the colour-blocking (intarsia) technique, work each area of colour with a separate small ball of yarn, and when changing colours twist the yarns at back of work to avoid a hole.

Working from the chart
The large square on the chart is 29 stitches wide and 40 rows tall, and the smaller inner square is 9 stitches wide by 13 rows tall. When working from the chart, read all odd-numbered (knit) rows from right to left and all even-numbered (purl) rows from left to right.

To make the cushion-cover front

Using the knit cast-on, cast on 87 sts, joining in colours as follows – 29C, 29B, 29A.

Squares row 1

With same side of work still facing, beg patt as follows:

Row 1 (RS) K across row, using colours for the squares in chart row 1 as follows – 29A, 29B, 29C.

Row 2 P across row, using colours for chart row 2 as follows – 29C, 29B, 29A.

Rows 3–12 [Rep rows 1 and 2] 5 times.

Row 13 Rep row 1.

Row 14 P across row, using colours as follows – 10C, 9E, 10C, 10B, 9D, 10B, 10A, 9C, 10A.

Row 15 K across row, using colours as follows – 10A, 9C, 10A, 10B, 9D, 10B, 10C, 9E, 10C.

Rows 16–25 [Rep rows 14 and 15] 5 times.

Row 26 Rep row 14.

Rows 27–40 [Rep rows 1 and 2] 7 times.

This completes the first row of two-colour squares, so ending with RS facing for next row.

Squares rows 2 and 3

Following the chart, work squares rows 2 and 3 as set, but following the colour diagram for colours. Cast off purlwise, using the same colours as the last row.

To finish the cushion-cover front

Weave in any loose yarn ends.
Lay the work out flat and gently steam on the reverse to enhance the yarn.

To add the fabric cushion cover back

Cut a piece of fabric the same size as the knitted front plus 1.5cm (¹⁄₂in) extra all around for the seam allowance.

With right sides together, pin the cushion-cover front to the fabric along the seam lines, easing to fit. Using matching thread and a sewing needle, stitch the knitted front to the fabric back piece around three sides.

Turn the cushion cover right side out. Insert the cushion pad and sew the remaining side closed.

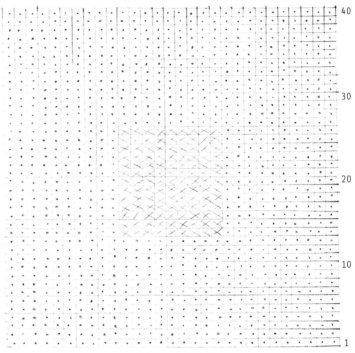

patt repeat = 29 sts

☐ background colour
☒ centre square colour

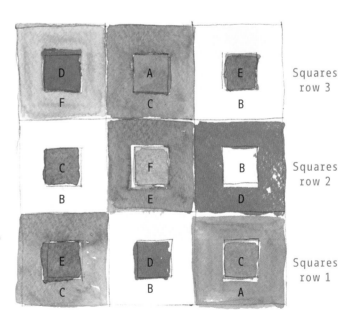

Squares row 3

Squares row 2

Squares row 1

17 Spots Cushions

The spots are worked on a light background on one of these two cushions and the other uses exactly the same colours but has a dark background – a simple colour trick that always works. The beautiful wool-silk yarn not only takes colour well but gives great stitch definition.

Skill level

⬤⬛⬛☐
INTERMEDIATE

In this project you will learn...
Colour-blocking (intarsia) technique (see page 32); reading from a chart

Stitches used...
Stocking stitch

Materials
For both cushions
Super-fine-weight wool-silk yarn, such as Shibui
 Staccato (70% superwash merino wool, 30% silk;
 175m/191yd per 50g/1¾oz hank; **①** SUPER FINE)
 in the following 4 colours:
    A light silvery grey (Ash 2003) – 2 hanks
    B deep dusky plum (Velvet 2017) – 1 hank
    C dark rich brown (Grounds 2025) – 2 hanks
    D medium brown-grey (Mineral 2022) – 1 hank
Pair of 2.75mm (US size 2) knitting needles
Large blunt-tipped sewing needle
50cm (½yd) of a plain shiny fabric, for each back
Sewing needle and matching sewing thread, for
 fabric back
Two square feather cushion pads, 32cm x 32cm
 (13in x 13in)

Note: Yarn amounts given are based on average requirements and are approximate.

Size
Each cushion measures approximately 32cm x 32cm (13in x 13in)

Tension
28 sts and 38 rows to 10cm (4in) square measured over st st using 2.75mm (US size 2) needles. Use larger or smaller needles if necessary to obtain the correct tension.

Abbreviations
See page 143.

Notes
Working the colour pattern
Using the colour-blocking (intarsia) technique, work each area of colour with a separate small ball of yarn, and when changing colours twist the yarns at back of work to avoid a hole.

Working from the chart
When working from the chart, read all odd-numbered (knit) rows from right to left and all even-numbered (purl) rows from left to right.

To make the cushion-cover front
Follow the first colour for the light version and
the colour in parentheses for the dark version.
Using A(C), cast on 90 sts.
Beg with a K row, work 6 rows in st st, so ending
RS facing for next row.
Place the first row of spots on the next row as
follows:
Row 7 (RS) K12A(C), yf, P6A(C), yb, K24A(C), K6D(D),
K24A(C), K6B(B), K12A(C). *90 sts*.
Row 8 P10A(C), P8B(B), P20A(C), P8D(D), P20A(C),
yb, K8A(C), yf, P10A(C). *90 sts*.
Cont in st st, following the chart for the coloured
spots and the rev st st textured spots, until chart
row 114 has been completed.
Cast off in A(C).

To finish the cushion-cover front
Weave in any loose yarn ends.
Lay the work out flat and gently steam on the
reverse to enhance the yarn.

To add the fabric cushion-cover back
Cut a piece of fabric the same size as the knitted
front plus 1.5cm (1/2in) extra all around for the
seam allowance.
With right sides together, pin the cushion-cover
front to the fabric along the seam lines, easing to
fit. Using matching thread and a sewing needle,
stitch the knitted front to the fabric back piece
around three sides.
Turn the cushion cover right side out. Insert the
cushion pad and sew the remaining side closed.

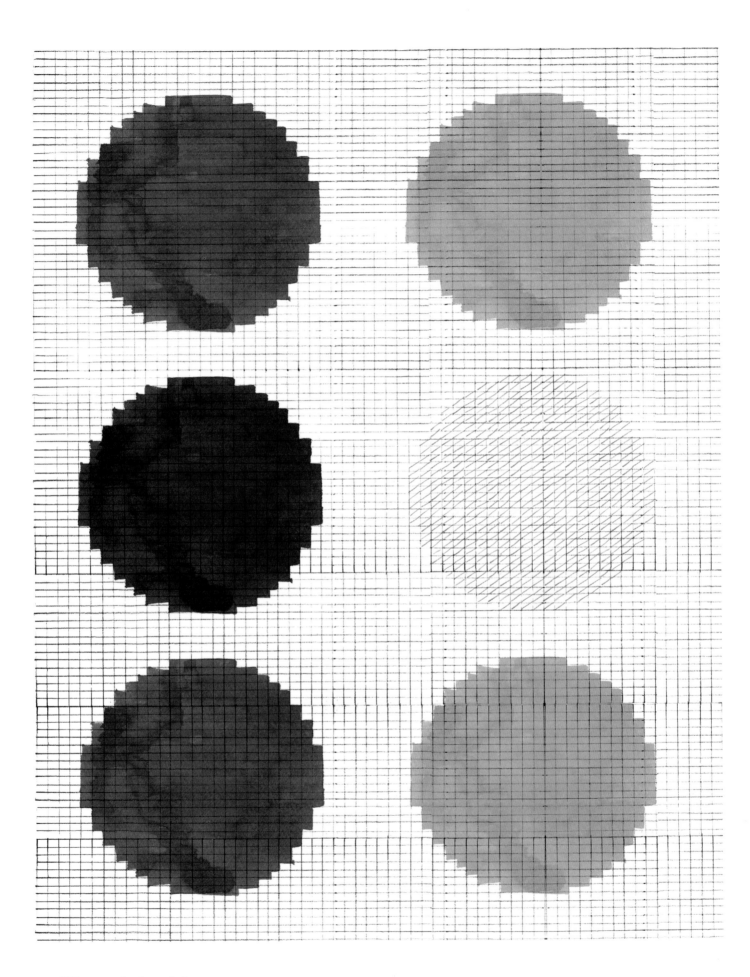

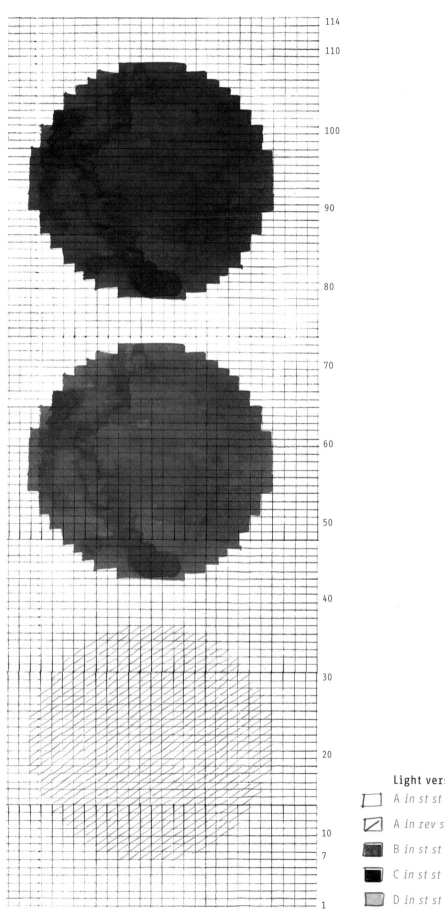

114
110
100
90
80
70
60
50
40
30
20
10
7
1

Light version	Dark version
A *in st st*	C *in st st*
A *in rev st st*	C *in rev st st*
B *in st st*	B *in st st*
C *in st st*	A *in st st*
D *in st st*	D *in st st*

18 Spotty Blanky

Worked in three colours using the double-knitting technique, this spot pattern creates a contemporary reversible baby blanket. The instructions are for a back and front in the same pattern in reversed colours, but feel free to vary the pattern on the back like I did.

Skill level

■■■■ ▬
EXPERIENCED

In this project you will learn...
Double-knitting technique; working from a chart

Stitches used...
Stocking stitch

Materials
Double-knitting-weight wool yarn, such as Erika Knight *British Blue Wool* (100% Blue-Faced Leicester wool; 55m/60yd per 25g/¾oz ball; **3** LIGHT) in the following 3 colours:
   A red (Mysore Red 051) – 6 balls
   B pale green (Leaf 045) – 5 balls
   C grey (Mouse 039) – 7 balls
4mm (US size 6) circular knitting needle, 100cm (40in) long
Large blunt-tipped sewing needle

Note: Yarn amounts given are based on average requirements and are approximate.

Size
Approximately 57cm x 53cm (22¾in x 21¼in)

Tension
20 sts and 26 rows to 10cm (4in) square measured over double-knit st st using 4mm (US size 6) needles. Use larger or smaller needles if necessary to obtain the correct tension.

Abbreviations
See page 143.

Note
Working the double-knitting fabric
The double-knitting technique creates two layers of stocking stitch fabric situated back to back with their wrong or purl sides facing each other and their right or knit sides facing out. The two pieces are connected at the cast-on edge and the sides but entirely separate throughout the centre, just like two sides of a pocket.
When the fabric is a solid colour one ball of yarn is used for each layer, and for the 2-colour Fair Isle rows two balls are used for each layer.
This double fabric must be worked on a circular knitting needle (or double-pointed needles) as the work is not turned on the first row and the following alternate rows, but worked a second time in the same direction.
When turning the work, make sure the yarns are twisted around each other.

Slipping stitches on double-knitting
Slip all stitches purlwise.

To make the throw
Using C, cast on 228 sts – this will provide 114 sts for each side of the double fabric.
Begin the double-knitting, working each row twice in the same direction as follows:
Row 1a (front of fabric facing) Using A, *K1, yf, sl 1, yb; rep from * to end – slide sts back to other end of needle without turning work and beg next row with same side facing.
112 sts each side.
Row 1b (front of fabric facing) Using C, *yb, sl 1, yf, P1; rep from * to end – TURN work.
Row 2a (back of fabric facing) Using A, rep row 2 – slide sts back to other end of needle without

turning work and beg next row with same side facing.

Row 2b (back of fabric facing) Using C, rep row 1 – TURN work.

This completes the first 2 st st rows of the front layer in A and the first 2 st st rows of back layer in C, called '2 rows A(C)' – where A is the colour used for the front layer and C the colour used for the back layer.

Working 2 rows with the front of the fabric facing and 2 rows with the back of the work facing as set throughout, cont to form the st st stripe and spots pattern in reverse colours on the front and back as follows:

6 rows more A(C).

8 rows of small C(A) spots on A(C) background, following chart rows 2–9 and working any sts left after the 12th spot in background colour.

2 rows A(C).

2 rows B(C).

8 rows of small C(B) spots on B(C) background.

2 rows B(C).

22 rows A(C).

12 rows C(A).

2 rows A(C).

2 rows B(C).

10 rows of large C(B) spots on B(C) background, following chart rows 2–11 and working any sts left after the 10th spot in background colour.

4 rows B(C).

8 rows of small C(B) spots on B(C) background.

2 rows B(C).

2 rows A(C).

8 rows C(A).

2 rows A(C).

2 rows B(C).

12 rows C(B)

2 rows B(C).

2 rows A(C).

8 rows of small C(A) spots on A(C) background.

8 rows A(C).

Using A, cast off 2 sts at a time, by knitting through one front st and one back st with each st.

To finish

Weave in any loose yarn ends.
Lay the work out flat and gently steam on the reverse to enhance the yarn.

Small spots chart

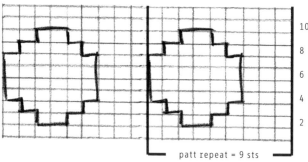

patt repeat = 9 sts

Large spots chart

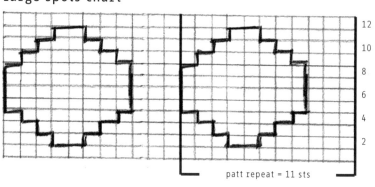

patt repeat = 11 sts

19 Coffee Cup Cosy

In colour blocking or 'intarsia' a separate ball or bobbin of yarn is used for each area of colour. This coffee cosy is a quick and easy project to try out this technique and also uses 'cheat's' intarsia or Swiss darning embroidery for the black lines.

Skill level

INTERMEDIATE

In the project you will learn...
Colour-blocking (intarsia) technique; Swiss darning (duplicate stitch) embroidery

Stitches used
Stocking stitch; K1, P1 rib

Materials
Aran-weight wool yarn, such as Erika Knight *Vintage Wool* (100% pure British wool; 87m/95yd per 50g/1¾oz hank; (4) MEDIUM) in the following 7 colours:
   A pale beige (Flax) – 1 hank
   B grey (Drizzle) – 1 hank
   C dark grape (Mulberry) – 1 hank
   D aqua (Leighton) – 1 hank
   E fuchsia (Gorgeous) – 1 hank
   F dark blue (Dark) – 1 hank
   G black (Pitch) – 1 hank
Pair of 4.5mm (US size 7) knitting needles
Large blunt-tipped sewing needle

Size
To fit average-size 'take away' paper coffee cup

Tension
18½ sts and 26 rows to 10cm (4in) square measured over color pattern using 4.5mm (US size 7) needles. Use larger or smaller needles if necessary to obtain the correct tension.

Abbreviations
See page 143.

Notes
Working from a chart
Work the diamonds colour pattern in stocking stitch following the chart (omitting the black rakers). Use the colour-blocking (intarsia) technique and read odd-numbered (knit) chart rows from right to left and even-numbered (purl) chart rows from left to right. See page 32 for how to work colour blocking.

Working the Swiss darning
Use Swiss darning (duplicate stitch) to embroider the black 'criss cross' or 'rakers' onto the finished diamond pattern. See pages 34–35 for how to work Swiss darning.

To make the cup cosy

Using A, cast on 42 sts.

Work 3 rows in K1, P1 rib.

Beg with a K row, work 2 rows in st st, so ending with RS facing for next row.

Using the intarsia method and six colours (A, B, C, D, E and F), introduce chart patt on next rows as follows:

Row 1 (RS) K1A; K 40 sts of chart row 1 across next 40 sts as follows – 3A, 2F, 6A, 2E, 6A, 2D, 6A, 2C, 6A, 2B, 3A; K1A.

Row 2 P1A; P 40 sts of chart row 2 across next 40 sts as follows – 3A, 2B, 6A, 2C, 6A, 2D, 6A, 2E, 6A, 2F, 3A; P1A.

Last 2 rows set position of chart.

Cont diamond patt following rows 3–14 of chart **and at the same time** inc 1 st at each end of row 5 and row 11. *46 sts.*

Using A, work 2 rows in st st.

Work 3 rows in K1, P1 rib.

Cast off in rib.

To finish

Weave in any loose yarn ends.

Lay the work out flat and gently steam on the reverse to enhance the yarn, avoiding the ribbing.

Following the chart and using G (black), Swiss darn (duplicate stitch) the rakers across the diamonds.

Sew the side seam using an invisible stitch.

A *in st st*

B *in st st*

C *in st st*

D *in st st*

E *in st st*

F *in st st*

G *in Swiss darning*

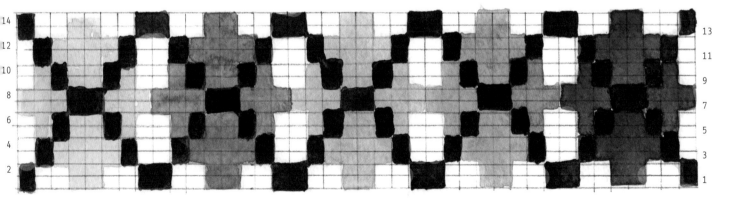

20 Plaid Rose Cushion

To add layers of pattern to your colour knitting, simply select a bold fabric pattern, photocopy it, enlarge or reduce it to suit your design and trace it onto knitter's chart paper. Then work it and vertical stripes in Swiss darning onto the knitting.

Skill level

INTERMEDIATE

In this project you will learn...
How to change colours; Swiss darning embroidery

Stitches used...
Stocking stitch

Materials
Fine-weight cotton yarn, such as Rowan *Cotton Glacé* (100% mercerised cotton; 115m/125yd per 50g/1¾oz ball; ② FINE) in the following 10 colours:
- A bright pink (Bubbles 724) – 2 balls
- B dark red (Blood Orange 445) – 1 ball
- C plum (Garnet 841) – 1 ball
- D light grey (Dawn Grey 831) – 1 ball
- E bright yellow (Mineral 856) – 1 ball
- F pale yellow (Ochre 833) – 1 ball
- G pale orange (Persimmon 832) – 1 ball
- H black (Black 727) – 1 ball
- I pale green (Shoot 814) – 1 ball
- J bright blue (Aqua 858) – 1 ball

Pair of 3.75mm (US size 5) knitting needles
Large blunt-tipped sewing needle
50cm (½yd) of a cotton fabric print, for back
Sewing needle and matching sewing thread, for fabric back
Square feather cushion pad, 45cm x 45cm (18in x 18in)

Note: Yarn amounts given are based on average requirements and are approximate.

Size
Approximately 44.5cm x 44.5cm (17¾in x 17¾in)

Tension
21½ sts and 30 rows to 10cm (4in) measured over st st using 3.75mm (US size 5) needles. Use larger or smaller needles if necessary to obtain the correct tension.

Abbreviations
See page 143.

Notes
Joining in a new colour for stripes
On the row before you need the new colour, work to the last stitch. Taking the end of the new colour, use together with the yarn in work to work the last stitch, creating a 'double stitch'. On the first stitch of next row, work the double stitch as one stitch with just the end of the new colour. This will securely 'anchor' your new yarn and neither create unsightly knots nor create bumps.

Working the Swiss darning
Use Swiss darning (duplicate stitch) to embroider the rose and leaves and the vertical lines onto the striped knitting. See pages 34–35 for how to work Swiss darning.

To make the cushion-cover front
Using A, cast on 96 sts.
Beg with a K row, work in st st using the stripe sequence as follows:
A 10 rows
C 1 row
B 3 rows
A 30 rows
C 1 row
[B 1 row, C 1 row] 9 times
B 24 rows
A 11 rows
C 1 row
B 3 rows
A 30 rows
Cast off.

To embellish
Using the small chart, Swiss darn the leaf motif, with the colours indicated, in the bottom left-hand corner of the knitting. Position the motif so that the first row of leaf stitches are 2 rows up from the bottom of the knitting and the leaf tip at the left edge is 2 stitches in from the left side edge of the knitting.
Using the big chart, Swiss darn the rose and leaves motif, with the colours indicated, at the top right-hand side of the knitting. Position the motif so that the tip of the top leaf is 2 rows down from the top edge of the knitting and the right edge of the motif is 2 stitches from the right side edge of the knitting.
Swiss darn the 2-stitch-wide vertical lines in J and D. Position the centre line 48 stitches in from right-hand edge, the left line 16 sts in from left-hand edge (starting where the leaf finished), and the right line 15 sts in from right-hand edge in the areas without the motif.

To finish the the cushion-cover front
Weave in any loose yarn ends.
Lay the work out flat and gently steam on the reverse to enhance the yarn.

To add the fabric cushion-cover back
Cut a piece of fabric the same size as the knitted front plus 1.5cm (1⁄2in) extra all around for the seam allowance.
With right sides together, pin the cushion-cover front to the fabric along the seam lines, easing to fit. Using matching thread and a sewing needle, stitch the knitted front to the fabric back piece around three sides.
Turn the cushion cover right side out. Insert the cushion pad and sew the remaining side closed.

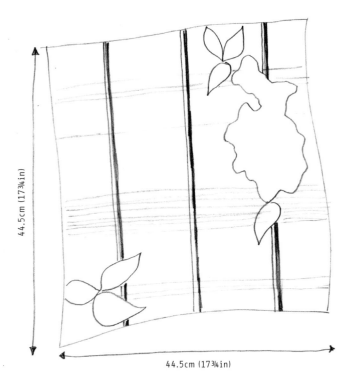

44.5cm (17¾in)

44.5cm (17¾in)

E

F

G

H

I

J

Recommended yarns

There is a yarn specified for each of the twenty designs in the Project Workshops section of this book. If you stick to the recommended yarn, you just need to pick your preferred shades. However, if you want to use a different yarn to the one specified, you need to compare the tensions given to ensure the finished result will not differ too wildly.

There are standard weights – or thicknesses – of yarns, recognised throughout the spinner's industry. Hand-knit yarns commonly range from 4ply through double knitting to super chunky at the opposite end of the scale. Within each of these categories there is a degree of tolerance, so it is still important to check the tension of each yarn against that given in a pattern. The weight categories listed with the yarns for the projects (1 super fine, 2 fine, 3 light, 4 medium, 5 bulky and 6 super bulky) have been determined by the weight categories recognised by the Craft Yarn Council of America. If using a substitute yarn, use these categories as a helpful guide.

Each yarn will have slightly varying physical properties from the next and will perform differently. Some yarns may be colourfast and easycare whilst others may only be suitable for dry-cleaning or could possibly felt if not treated correctly. The care information for a yarn will be given on the yarn label that comes with the yarn – it is either a paper band wrapped around the ball, skein or hank, or a paper tag tied to the yarn. I always keep a yarn label for each project that I make – and if I give a hand knit as a gift, I include the yarn label so the recipient knows how to care for the item. When you invest so much of your time and energy into creating a hand-knitted item, great care should be taken in the laundering.

Alongside the manufacturer's brand name and the name given to the specific yarn, a yarn label will typically carry the following information:

Average tension and recommended needle sizes
This is the spinner's recommended tension and needle size. A designer may vary from this recommendation within a pattern. If so, always go with the designer's recommendation.

Weight of yarn balls and hanks
Most yarns come in either 50-gram (1¾-ounce) or 100-gram (3½-ounce) balls or hanks.

Meterage (yardage)
This is the length of yarn in the ball. It is just as important to consider as tension when purchasing a substitute yarn. Always purchase a substitute yarn by how many metres (yards) you need rather than by how many grams (ounces).

Fibre composition
A ball band will list the materials that the yarn is made from, whether that is 100% pure wool or a blend of fibres such as cotton and silk. This affects not just the method of care for the finished item, but also the suitability of a yarn for a certain project.

Shade and dye-lot numbers
Each shade of yarn is given an identifying name and/or number by the manufacturer. When purchasing yarn the dye-lot number is equally, if not more important, as this number needs to be the same on every ball. As yarn is dyed in batches, buying yarn with the same dye-lot numbers ensures there will be no colour variations between balls.

Care instructions
A ball band will indicate whether the yarn is suitable for machine washing or is dry-clean only, and whether or not it can be ironed and, if so, at what temperature. This information is usually given in the form of standard fabric-care symbols.

The following are the specifications for all the yarns used in this book:

Erika Knight *British Blue Wool* **(3)** LIGHT
A double-knitting-weight wool yarn; 100% Blue-Faced Leicester wool; 55m/60yd per 25g/¾oz; 22 sts sts x 30 rows per 10cm/4in over st st using 4mm (US size 6) needles.

Erika Knight *Fur Wool* **(6)** SUPER BULKY
A super-chunky-weight wool 'fur' yarn; 97% wool, 3% nylon binder; 40m/44yd per 100g/3½oz hank; 5½ sts x 8 rows per 10cm/4in over st st using 15mm (US size 19) needles.

Erika Knight *Maxi Wool* **(6)** SUPER BULKY
A super-chunky-weight wool yarn; 100% British wool; 80m/87yd per 100g/3½oz hank; 8 sts x 12 rows per 10cm/4in over st st using 12mm (US size 17) needles.

Erika Knight *Vintage Wool* **(4)** MEDIUM
An aran-weight wool yarn; 100% British wool; 87m/95yd per 50g/1¾oz hank; 18 sts x 24 rows per 10cm/4in over st st using 5mm (US size 8) needles.

Isager *Alpaca 2* **(1)** SUPER FINE
A super-fine-weight wool-alpaca yarn; 50% merino lambswool, 50% baby alpaca; 247m/270yd per 50g/1¾oz; 26 sts rows per 10cm/4in over st st using 3mm (US size 3) needles.

Lana Knits *Allhemp6* **(3)** LIGHT
A double-knitting-weight hemp yarn; 100% hemp; 150m/165yd per 100g/3½oz hank; 22 sts per 10cm/4in over st st using 3.75mm (US size 5) needles.

Abbreviations

Madeline Tosh *Tosh DK* 3 LIGHT
A double-knitting-weight hand-dyed wool yarn; 100% superwash merino wool; 206m/225yd per 100g/3¹⁄₂oz hank; 20–22 sts per 10cm/4in over st st using 4–4.5mm (US size 6–7) needles.

Rowan *Cocoon* 5 BULKY
A chunky-weight wool-mohair yarn; 80% merino wool, 20% kid mohair; 115m/126yd per 100g/3¹⁄₂oz ball; 14 sts x 16 rows per 10cm/4in over st st using 7mm (US size 10¹⁄₂) needles.

Rowan *Cotton Glacé* 2 FINE
A fine-weight cotton yarn; 100% mercerised cotton; 115m/125yd per 50g/1³⁄₄oz ball; 23 sts x 32 rows per 10cm/4in over st st using 3.25mm (US size 3) needles.

Rowan *Creative Linen* 3 LIGHT
A double-knitting-weight linen-cotton yarn; 50% linen, 50% cotton; 200m/219yd per 100g/3¹⁄₂oz hank; 21 sts x 28 rows per 10cm/4in over st st using 4.5mm (US size 7) needles.

Shibui *Staccato* 1 SUPER FINE
A super-fine-weight wool-silk yarn; 70% superwash merino wool, 30% silk; 175m/191yd per 50g/1³⁄₄oz hank; 28–32 sts per 10cm/4in over st st using 2.25–2.75mm (US size 1–2) needles.

The following are the abbreviations used in this book. Any special abbreviations are given with individual patterns.

alt	alternate
beg	begin(ning)
cm	centimetre(s)
cont	continu(e)(ing)
dec	decreas(e)(ing)
foll	follow(s)(ing)
g	gram(s)
in	inch(es)
inc	increase(e)(ing)
K	knit
m	metre(s)
M1	make one st; pick up strand between st just knit and next st with tip of left needle and work into back of it (to increase 1 st)
mm	millimetre(s)
oz	ounce(s)
P	purl
patt	pattern; or work in pattern
psso	pass slipped stitch over
rem	remain(s)(ing)
rep	repeat(s)(ing)
rev st st	reverse stocking stitch
RS	right side
sl	slip
st(s)	stitch(es)
st st	stocking stitch
tbl	through back of loop(s)
tog	together
WS	wrong side
yb	yarn to back of work between two needles
yd	yard(s)
yf	yarn to front of work between two needles
* [ ]	Repeat instructions after asterisk, between asterisks or inside square brackets as many times as instructed.

Knitting needle sizes
The closest equivalent sizes across three needle-sizing systems – UK metric, US and old UK (imperial) follow.

Metric	US	Old UK	Metric	US	Old UK
15mm	19	–	4.5mm	7	7
12mm	17	–	4mm	6	8
10mm	15	000	3.75mm	5	9
9mm	13	00	3.5mm	4	–
8mm	11	0	3.25mm	3	10
7.5mm	–	1	3mm	–	11
7mm	–	2	2.75mm	2	12
6.5mm	10¹⁄₂	3	2.5mm	–	–
6mm	10	4	2.25mm	1	13
5.5mm	9	5	2mm	0	14
5mm	8	6			

Acknowledgements

Simple Colour Knitting has been a long time in the making, a somewhat elongated journey, with many bumps and detours along the way, which have altered, refined and framed the final product. Colour is a constant journey, it refreshes ones creative spirit like nothing else, always changing with light, space and mood. Colour is intrinsic to who we are and to how we interpret our environment. Colour is the inspiration and stimulus to my personal creative process and the journey of putting this book together has indeed been a colourful one.

It has involved the very best people of the highest calibre with the most discerning eyes, exacting standards, meticulous attention to detail and most of all unbelievable patience in working with me. For all of which I am enormously grateful and I would like to extend my heartfelt thanks and appreciation for their huge contributions. It is a privilege to work with all of them and most certainly this book would not have happened without them.

I am forever appreciative of my long association with Quadrille Publishing. And most especially with Jane O'Shea, my publishing director, who since the beginning has championed me. No one has the ability to chastise and encourage with such style. I have tried and challenged the patience of my creative editor Lisa Pendreigh beyond question and her professionalism, unwavering support, innate creative talents, perception and perseverance is faultless. She is simply the best. Vast thanks to Claire Peters, for surpassing my vision of the concept for this book, with her creative design and glorious watercolour illustrations. And to Vincent Smith and his team for the exceptional production.

I am indebted to Sally Harding for her huge contribution to this book, for her inestimable and meticulous endeavour in checking the patterns and text. She is a one-stop shop for all things knit and crochet, and thank goodness for that.

I am thrilled to have Yuki Sugiura to photograph the book, her innate yet ease of style is inherent to the sensibility of this book, and of course huge thanks to Kim Lightbody for assisting. It was fabulous to have stylist Holly Bruce, a whirlwind of enthusiasm and energy to collate and create for us. Chinh Hoang, huge thanks for being so elegantly and effortlessly beautiful. Sincerest thanks to Simon Kämpfer, a hugely talented designer of exquisite furniture, who went the extra mile so we would have the most beautiful pieces which elevated the projects far beyond the humble handmade, and to Simon's studio for loaning the pieces.

Enduring gratitude and thanks to Sally Lee, my creative practitioner, for her immense contribution to this book, her expertise, diligence and pragmatism are rare and greatly appreciated. And to a small but perfectly selected team of design sample knitters and makers, most especially Faye Perriam, Jools Yeo, Eileen Maccabe and Lucyna Coyne. And to Amelia Bur who made invaluable contributions during her internship with me.

To Kate Buller of Rowan Yarns, Amy Hendrix of MadeleineTosh, Darcy Cameron of Shibui, Lana Hames of LanaKnits, and Isager, my huge thanks for creating inspirational and exceptional yarns of the highest quality and, invaluably, for their generosity in contributing yarns for the projects and support of this book.

Finally and fundamentally to Bella, my daughter, and now collaborator in the Erika Knight Yarn Collection. She has always said, "It's in her genes." I have no words (for once) to express my thanks, appreciation, gratitude and respect in all that she is, what she does for me, and getting us here.

And finally this book is dedicated to those who love colour and creating and CRAFT.

Publisher's Acknowledgements
The publisher would like to thank the following for loaning accessories and other items:

BRICKETT DAVDA
www.brickettdavda.com
The yarn bowls on page 112 are made by Brickett Davda exclusively for Erika Knight. For further information, contact info@erikaknight.co.uk.

DE LA ESPADA
www.delaespada.com

SIMON KÄMPFER
www.simonkaempfer.com

VOLGA LINEN
www.volgalinen.co.uk